The Social Web in the Hotel Industry

Nadine Chehimi

The Social Web in the Hotel Industry

The Impact of the Social Web on the Information Process of German Hotel Guests

Springer Gabler

Nadine Chehimi
Trier, Germany

Dissertation, Universität Trier, 2013

ISBN 978-3-658-04543-2 ISBN 978-3-658-04544-9 (eBook)
DOI 10.1007/978-3-658-04544-9

The Deutsche Nationalbibliothek lists this publication in the Deutsche Nationalbibliografie; detailed bibliographic data are available in the Internet at http://dnb.d-nb.de.

Library of Congress Control Number: 2013955878

Springer Gabler

Printed on acid-free paper

Springer Gabler is a brand of Springer DE.
Springer DE is part of Springer Science+Business Media.
www.springer-gabler.de

Chehimi, Nadine

vom Fachbereich VI Geographie/Geowissenschaften
der Universität Trier zur Verleihung des akademischen Grades
‚Doktor der Philosophie' (Dr. phil.) genehmigte Dissertation

The Social Web in the Hotel Industry

The Impact of the Social Web on the Information Process of German Hotel Guests

Betreuender und Berichterstattender: Univ.-Prof. Dr. Andreas Kagermeier

Berichterstattende: Univ.-Prof. Dr. Ulrike Sailer

Datum der wissenschaftlichen Aussprache: 13. Februar 2013

Trier 2013

Leicht modifizierte Fassung

Danksagung

Ich danke ganz herzlich Herrn Professor Dr. Kagermeier für die Anregungen und Betreuung dieser Dissertation.

Mein Dank gilt auch Frau Professor Dr. Sailer für die freundliche Übernahme der Zweitkorrektur.

Meiner Familie und meinen Freunden danke ich für ihre Unterstützung.

Zusammenfassung

Zusammenfassung der vom Fachbereich VI Geographie/Geowissenschaften der Universität Trier zur Verleihung des akademischen Grades ‚Doktor der Philosophie' (Dr. phil.) genehmigten englischsprachigen Dissertation mit dem Titel **The Social Web in the Hotel Industry. The Impact of the Social Web on the Information Process of German Hotel Guests** von Nadine Chehimi, M.A. (FH).

Im Zentrum der Dissertation steht das Social Web. Dieses wird als sozialer Teilbereich des Internets verstanden, der es fremden Nutzern ermöglicht, interaktiv miteinander zu kommunizieren und dadurch der sozialen Kontaktpflege und dem -aufbau dient. Die Bedeutung des Social Web geht mittlerweile weit über diesen ursprünglichen Fokus hinaus und schließt heute auch unternehmerische und kommerzielle Aktivitäten mit ein. Die Zielsetzung der vorliegenden Arbeit ist es herauszufinden, inwieweit das Social Web Einfluss auf die Informationssuche deutscher Hotelgäste nimmt.

Um ein Verständnis für die komplexe Thematik des Social Web zu schaffen, wird zunächst auf die Entstehung und Entwicklung desselbigen eingegangen. Die Reichweite und Vielfältigkeit des Social Web wird durch die Präsentation verschiedener Social Web Anwendungen im Allgemeinen und touristischer Anwendungen im Speziellen dargestellt. Zudem erfolgt eine situative Beschreibung der unternehmerischen Nutzung des Social Web, die auch eine Übersicht über die damit verbundenen Chancen und Risiken gibt. Da die Auswirkung des Social Web auf die touristische Informationssuche Gegenstand der Untersuchung ist, werden anschließend allgemeine und touristische Informationstheorien präsentiert. Zudem wird ein Modell vorgestellt, das für den weiteren Verlauf der Arbeit als Bezugsgröße dient. Anschließend erfolgt eine Sekundäranalyse zu bereits durchgeführten Studien über die touristische Bedeutung des Social Web. Da die Dissertation in das Umfeld der Hotelindustrie eingebettet ist, erfolgt als letzte theoretische Grundlage die Skizzierung des deutschen Hotelmarkts. Der methodologische Teil umfasst die Analyse zur Wahl einer geeigneten Erhebungsmethode, die letztlich auf einen standardisierten online Gästefragebogen fällt sowie die Präsentation des Fallbeispiels: einer Hotelkette mit mehreren Hotels in Deutschland.

Abschließend werden die Untersuchungsergebnisse zusammenfassend dargestellt:

- **Informative Nutzung des Social Web**
  Als relevante Seiten für die Suche nach Hotelinformationen werden vorwiegend Hotel-Bewertungsseiten wie TripAdvisor und Buchungsseiten mit Bewertungsfunktion wie HRS identifiziert. Auch soziale Netzwerke wie Facebook,

Reisecommunities wie TripsByTips und Foto- und Videoportale wie YouTube dienen der Informationssuche. Podcasts, Blogs und Microblogs werden während der Informationssuche vernachlässigt.
Die gezielte Suche nach hotelrelevanten Informationen wird vorwiegend von Gästen betrieben, die das Social Web auch insgesamt regelmäßig nutzen. Sogenannte *Rand Nutzer*, die nur äußerst sporadisch im Social Web surfen, greifen vorwiegend nicht auf dieses Informationsmedium zurück. Daher können im Social Web weitestgehend Gäste erreicht werden, die eine regelmäßige Social Web Nutzung vorweisen. Die Möglichkeit zur Kommunikation mit dem gesamten Gästeklientel ist somit nicht gegeben. Für die Nutzung des Social Web als Informationsmedium ist es i.d.R. unerheblich, ob es sich um Gelegenheits- oder Vielreisende handelt. Mit Ausnahme von Hotelbewertungsseiten und Buchungsseiten mit Bewertungsfunktion greifen beide gleichermaßen auf das Social Web zu Informationszwecken zurück.

- **Altersübergreifende Nutzung des Social Web**
  Auch sogenannte *Best Ager*, die für die Arbeit mit einem Alter ab 56 Jahren definiert wurden, nutzen das Social Web als Informationsmedium. Auch wenn der Großteil der Best Ager angab, das Social Web insgesamt nicht zu nutzen und somit hier auch keine Informationssuche stattfinden kann, nutzen Best Ager, die im Social Web aktiv sind, dasselbige auch zu Informationszwecken. Im Vergleich zu der jüngeren Zielgruppe konnten in der informativen Nutzung keine großen Unterschiede festgestellt werden; in einigen Fällen zeigten Best Ager sogar eine höhere Social Web Affinität, z.B. hinsichtlich der aktiven Berichterstattung nach dem Hotelaufenthalt. Best Ager können somit durchaus, wenn auch in vergleichsweise geringerem Maße, im Social Web erreicht werden.

- **Auswirkungen des Social Web auf die eigene Buchungsentscheidung**
  Erfahrungsberichte fremder User nehmen signifikant Einfluss auf die persönliche Buchungsentscheidung. Hierbei spielen Bewertungen auf Hotel-Bewertungsportalen und Buchungsseiten mit Bewertungsfunktion die größte Rolle, aber auch Kommentare in Reisecommunities, sozialen Netzwerken und Foto- und Videoportalen beeinflussen die Buchungsentscheidung. Besonders stark ist der Einfluss von Bewertungen auf regelmäßige Social Web User. Der Einfluss erstreckt sich i.d.R. gleichermaßen auf Viel- und Gelegenheitsreisende.

- **Entwicklung des Social Web als Distributionskanal**
  Die Akzeptanz von *Social Bookings* (Möglichkeit zur Hotelbuchung auf Social Web Seiten) ist insgesamt eher zurückhaltend. Werden jedoch nur die Gäste betrachtet, die im Social Web nach Informationen für ihre nächste Hotelübernachtung suchen, wird eine deutlich positivere Haltung bemerkbar. Besonders stark ist dieser Zusammenhang bei sozialen Netzwerken ausgeprägt.

- **Empfindung von Werbung im Social Web**
  Der Einsatz von *Social Advertising* (Werbung im Social Web) wird insgesamt eher neutral empfunden und nur eine kleine Teilmenge klickt auf entsprechende Werbebanner. Wird jedoch berücksichtigt, inwiefern das Social Web als Informationsquelle genutzt wird, ist eine positivere Wahrnehmung bei den Nutzern, die sich im Social Web informieren, zu bemerken.

Somit identifiziert die Arbeit die wesentlichen Aspekte der Hotelinformationssuche, die durch das Social Web beeinflusst werden. Diese Erkenntnisse dürfen jedoch nicht auf alle Hotelgäste übertragen werden. Auch wenn die Zuwachsraten der Social Web Nutzung in den letzten Jahren stark gestiegen sind und von einer positiven Zukunftsentwicklung ausgegangen werden kann, wird momentan nur ein Teilbereich der Gäste, nämlich der Social Web Nutzer, vom Social Web beeinflusst. Dies muss bei der Analyse zur Bedeutung des Social Web berücksichtigt werden. Zudem liefert die Arbeit nur Kenntnisse für die Hotelbranche; die Ergebnisse sind daher nicht ohne weiteres auf andere touristische Dienstleistungen zu übertragen.

Summary

Summary of the dissertation **The Social Web in the Hotel Industry. The Impact of the Social Web on the Information Process of German Hotel Guests**, approved by the Faculty VI Geographie/Geowissenschaften of the University of Trier for the award of the academic degree ‘Doktor der Philosophie’ (Dr. phil.), submitted by Nadine Chehimi, M.A. (FH).

The focus of the dissertation is the social web, which is defined as the social part of the Internet that enables (personally unknown) people to socially interact with each other in order to cherish friendships and make new acquaintances. The social web's current significance exceeds this initial focus, by also encompassing corporate and commercial activities. This dissertation examines to what extent the social web influences the information process of German hotel guests. In addition to the presentation of the social web's development and current state of use, general and tourist information processes as well as the German hotel market are described, in order to build a profound basis for the empirical study. The methodological part comprises the analysis of the appropriate research method, which results in applying a standardized online guest survey as well as the presentation of the sample case, which is a hotel chain with different hotels in Germany. Finally, the findings are presented:

- **Informational Social Web Usage:** Hotel review sites and booking sites with review function were identified as the most relevant sites during the information gathering. Additionally, social networks, travel communities and media sharing platforms are also accessed for retrieving information. Podcasts, blogs and microblogs are mainly not considered as a source of information. Predominantly, regular social web users access social web sites for the specific information search whereas users that use the social web very sporadically do mostly not consider it. With the exception of hotel review sites and booking sites with review function the social web is considered to be a source of information independent from travel frequency.
- **Social web usage across age:** The so-called *best agers*, who are defined as being older than 55 years, access the social web during the information gathering. Although the majority of best agers does not use the social web at all and does not consider it as an information source, those who stated that they use the social web accessed it also during information gathering. Hence, some best agers may access the social web as equally as the younger generation, sometimes even exceeding them, for example regarding the active contribution.

- **The impact of the social web on the booking decision:** Reviews of other users influence the personal booking decision significantly. The impact is especially strong of reviews on hotel review and booking sites. However, also reviews on travel communities, social networks and media sharing platforms are influencing factors. Frequent social web users are especially influenced.
- **Development of the social web into a distribution channel:** Generally, the acceptance of booking a hotel room on the social web is rather reluctant. However, among users that access the social web as a source of information the attitude is more positive, especially regarding bookings on social networks.
- **Perception of advertisements on the social web:**
  The overall attitude towards advertisements on the social web is neutral and only a small subset click on ad banners. However, when considering users that gather information on the social web, the attitude becomes more positive.

The dissertation highlights important aspects of the hotel information search, which are influenced by the social web. However, these findings may not be applied to all hotel guests, as the social web only influences the information process of guests using the social web. Hence, a great part remains unaffected, although the social web's growth rates of the last few years may forecast a positive development. Additionally, the paper presents only findings for the hotel information process and may therefore not be applicable to other tourist services.

Table of Contents

List of Tables

List of Figures

Abbreviation Index

ads	advertisements
AGOF	Arbeitsgemeinschaft Online Forschung
AIDA	attention, interest, decision, action
Ajax	asynchronous java script and XML
ANCOVA	analysis of covariance
ANOVA	analysis of variance
bl. & pod.	blogs & podcasts
book.s.w.rev.	booking sites with review function
BVDW	Bundesverband Digitale Wirtschaft e.V.
B2B	business-to-business
Cf.	confer
CRS	central reservation system
DEHOGA	Deutscher Hotel und Gaststättenverband e.V.
DIVSI	Deutsches Institut für Vertrauen und Sicherheit im Internet
e.g.	exempli gratia
e-tourism	electronic tourism
et al.	et alii
etc.	et cetera
f.	following
FAZ	Frankfurter Allgemeine Zeitung
fig.	figure
FTD	Financial Times Deutschland
GDP	gross domestic product
GDS	global distribution system
gen.	general
GPS	global positioning system
hot.rev.s.	hotel review sites
HTML	hype text markup language
IHA	Hotelverband Deutschland e.V.
imp.	impact
inf.	retrieving information
ISDN	Integrated Services Digital Network
m	million
med.shar.plat.	media sharing platforms
micr.bl	microblogs
p	probability of error
p.	page

pr	public relation
rep.	reporting
resp.	respectively
RH	research hypothesis
RSS	rich site summary, RDF site summary or really simple syndication
sms	short message sent
soc.book.acc.	social bookings acceptance
soc.net.	social networks
St.Can.Dis.Fun.Coefficient	standardized canonical discriminant function coefficient
st.dev.	standard deviation
tr.comm.	travel communities
TV	television
UGC	user-generated-content
URL	uniform resource locator
US	United States
USP	unique selling proposition
VIR	Verband Internet Reisen e.V.
vs.	versus
XML	extensible markup language
y.	years

1 Introduction

1.1 Problem Depiction

> *"I had a wonderful stay in this hotel. The food was excellent and the service outstanding. I can only recommend it."*

Until some years ago, this review would have only been shared with friends and families. The spread of the personal hotel experience would have been limited to the guest's circle of acquaintances and would have neither sustainably influenced the hotel's image nor the booking decision of many others. However, with the emergence of the social web, these personal and geographical limitations diminish. Today, guests can share their experiences with the whole online world. They can write reviews on review sites like TripAdvisor and HolidayCheck, they can upload photos on media sharing platforms like YouTube and can start discussions about their experiences on social networks like Facebook. All these sites belong to the so-called social web which has fundamentally changed the way users may gather information.[1] Users are no longer only consumers who access provider-based information but rather prosumers who actively create contents[2] – user-generated-content (UGC) – and are therefore also referred to as co-producers.[3]

The hotel industry belongs to the tourism sector which is characterized by a great need for consulting.[4] Therefore, this industry has always been very open to new information and communication technologies and nothing has influenced the tourism industry in the last 15 years more than the Internet.[5] While the Internet has already caused enormous changes in communication,[6] the social web may cause impacts of even vaster dimensions. In the past, hotels could decide which information they wanted to share. They could spread their messages via mass media and direct communication channels.[7] Hotels could determine the photos that were presented in their brochures and they could define the room layout that was published in tour operators' catalogues. Guests had to trust this information – mostly because not many other information sources existed. However, with the

1 Cf. Cornell University 2010, p. 5

2 Cf. Kagermeier 2011, p. 59, in: Boksberger et al. 2011

3 Cf. Bitkom.org 2010, p. 24

4 Cf. Lassnig 2010, p. 6, in: Lassnig et al. 2010

5 Cf. Lassnig 2010, p. 6, in: Lassnig et al. 2010

6 Cf. Feil et al. 2003, p. 429f., in: Becker et al. 2003

7 Cf. Schegg et al. 2010, p. 437, in: Gretzel et al. 2010

rise of the social web, users today can also consider reviews and personal experiences from other guests and thereby get information advantages.[8] Especially for tourist products, where the services cannot be tested before consumption,[9] this is of great benefit. The hotel's image is considerably influenced by the overall tone of the reviews[10] and the UGC is highly increasing market transparency.[11] The growth of the Internet and the emergence of the social web have fundamentally changed the way guests may gather and hotels may spread information.[12]

Usually, an overnight stay in a hotel is a service where the guest is directly affected by its quality. Especially tourist services which cannot be evaluated before consumption[13] carry a great risk.[14] Therefore, other people's personal experiences are a valuable source of information for one's own decision making process. With the help of review portals, social networks, travel communities and other applications, future guests are able to assess the hotel's services in advance, thereby minimizing the potential risk. With the rise of the social web, the traditional information sources are augmented by personal, user-generated reviews and comments: whereas formerly classic online information sources, e.g. the hotel website, were the main source of information for guests, social web sites are gaining more and more ground.[15] Generally, hotel review sites are the most frequently accessed online information source regarding the evaluation of accommodation alternatives.[16] The main reason for the great popularity of review sites may be the fact that tourist experiences are considered worth sharing.[17] However, the social web offers so much more than only review sites. It is therefore essential to know the degree of influence and consideration of the social web as a whole.

While the social web seems to be especially appealing to the so-called digital natives,[18] it may be an equally important information medium to the older genera-

8 Cf. Bitkom.org 2010, p. 2

9 Cf. Ip et al. 2010, p. 347, in: Gretzel et al. 2010

10 Cf. Schegg et al. 2010, p. 437, in: Gretzel et al. 2010

11 Cf. Schegg et al. 2010, p. 430, in: Gretzel et al. 2010

12 Cf. Xiang 2011, p. 343, in: Law et al. 2011

13 Cf. Ip et al. 2010, p. 347, in: Gretzel et al. 2010

14 Cf. Egger et al. 2010, p. 22, in: Lassnig et al. 2010

15 Cf. Schegg et al. 2010, p. 429, in: Gretzel et al. 2010

16 Cf. Marchiori et al. 2011, p. 101, in: Law et al. 2011

17 Cf. De Ascaniis et al. 2011, p. 125, in: Law et al. 2011

18 Users that did not have to learn the Internet's function but that were born into the online world are referred to as digital natives. (Cf. Prensky 2001, p.1)

tion. The so-called best agers[19] are identified as an interesting target group for the travel industry as they have plenty of leisure time and above-average incomes.[20] Best agers can be described as '[...] very sophisticated and wealthy [...] with high expectations'[21] and a highly distinctive loyalty.[22] Regarding the fact that the demographic trend will most likely create an increasing number of best agers in the future,[23] it is also essential to know whether and to what extent this target group can be reached via the social web. As best agers generally use the Internet and social web less than the younger generation, they may be easily neglected as an important target group.[24] However, when considering that most of the online growth is caused by users over the age of fifty,[25] the question arises if this also accounts for the use of the social web as an information source.[26]

The further scope of this paper will show that there is currently a great hype about the social web and many hotels are actively participating. However, the exact role the social web plays for hotel guests has not yet been defined. Although the importance of hotel review sites has unquestionably been acknowledged, the impact of the social web as a whole is still to be clarified. Therefore, this paper is dedicated to the analysis of the social web's effectiveness.

1.2 Objective

Against the background of increasing user numbers, growing hotel presence and services that have a high need for information, it is easy to make the assumption that the social web is a relevant factor for the hotel industry as it seems to be the perfect possibility for hotel guests to gather information. It is also from the hotels' point of view that the social web offers many opportunities. With their social web presence, hotels may enter into a dialogue with their guests, acquire new guests and intensify their relation with existing guests. Hotels may create consciousness

19 For this paper best agers are defined as people over the age of 55 years.

20 Cf. Zangerl et al. 2011, p. 75f., in: Law et al. 2011

21 Zangerl et al. 2011, p. 76, in: Law et al. 2011

22 Cf. Zangerl et al. 2011, p. 76, in: Law et al. 2011

23 Cf. Zangerl et al. 2011, p. 76, in: Law et al. 2011

24 Cf. Zangerl et al. 2011, p. 84, in: Law et al. 2011

25 Cf. van Eimeren et al. 2012, p. 378

26 The use of the social web as an information source is also referred to as informational social web usage or social information search in the following.

for their services in the guests' minds in order to be considered the next time guests evaluate different hotel choices. However, is the social web really used as an information source? Do future hotel guests consider reviews, Facebook fan pages and photos on YouTube when searching for information about their next hotel stay? Is it already a widespread phenomenon to search for personal experiences and reviews and does the social web already play an integrated part of the information search process? Or is it rather used randomly? If it is used, does it have a significant impact on the final booking decision? Which target groups can be reached on the social web? Can one define a certain user typology that is relying on the social web, a so-called social information seeker, or is the social web frequented independently from the user characteristics? **To what extent does the social web influence the hotel guest's information search?**

This paper seeks to determine the social web's exact role. The findings of the study are, on one hand, to reveal the impact and consequences of the social web on the guest's information process and, on the other hand, to provide hotels with valuable information for their communication strategy on the social web. With this aim in mind, the following research hypotheses (RH) have been defined:

RH I: The informational social web usage depends on travel frequency and the general social web usage.

The aim of RH I is to elaborate whether there are differences in the usage of the social web as a hotel information medium when comparing frequent and occasional hotel guests and frequent and occasional general social web users.

RH II: The informational social web usage differs between the younger generation and best agers.

A common assumption about the social web user characteristics concerns the age as the general opinion prevails that predominantly young people use it. If this assumption holds true, the consequence is that mostly younger users integrate the social web into their information search process, which, in turn, means that mainly younger hotel guests can be approached via the social web and that the communication should concentrate on them. It would also imply that best agers are hardly to be reached via the social web. Therefore, both user groups are compared and analyzed in RH II in order to give recommendations for a target group-appropriate approach on the social web.

RH III: The varying social web sites have a different impact on the personal hotel booking decision.

RH III presumes that the importance of the social web as an information source cannot be generalized but needs to be considered according to the individual types of social web applications. Whereas some applications may have a crucial importance to certain users, other sites may be neglected.

RH IV: The social web has the potential to evolve into a relevant distribution channel.

RH IV aims to prove whether the social web does not only have the potential to influence the information process of hotel guests but also the distribution policies of hotels by implementing booking possibilities on social web sites.

RH V: The perception of social advertising depends on particular user characteristics.

Placing advertisements on social web sites – social advertising – is becoming more and more popular for hotels as potential guests can be acquired in their familiar surroundings: on websites where they spend increasingly more of their leisure time. RH V looks at how exactly ads on social web sites are perceived by users and if there are distinct user characteristics responsible for a positive or negative perception.

1.3 Structure and Procedure

The paper has been organized in the following way:

Fig. 1: Structure of the Paper. Source: own survey

While chapter 1 provides an introduction to the topic area, chapter 2 is dedicated to the social web. Its beginning, development and the current number of its users are presented in detail in order to build a profound basis for the further discussions. Chapter 3 deals with general information theories and also reviews the secondary literature to give an overview of the current state of knowledge. In chapter 4, the German hotel market is described in order to properly classify the environment of the study. The methodology of this study is shown in chapter 5. Chapter 6 presents the findings of this study. Finally, concluding remarks are given in chapter 7.

2 The Social Web

2.1 Definition

The emergence of the social web has fundamentally changed the online world. According to the Bundesverband Digitale Wirtschaft (BVDW), the world is currently in the biggest media revolution '[...] since the invention of modern letterpress printing by Gutenberg in 1452'.[27] Searching the keyword social web on Google reveals more than 1.87 billion results[28] – but what exactly is meant by this term? Web 2.0, social web, social media: all of these catchphrases describe the modified Internet usage of the last few years, however, their definition differs.

The term web 2.0 was made popular by Tim O'Reilly and Dale Dougherty in 2004, when they were looking for a title for their conference about the changing Internet.[29] Within a short time, web 2.0 became a popular catchphrase. It is defined by O'Reilly as follows: 'Web 2.0 is the network as platform, spanning all connected devices; web 2.0 applications are those that make the most of the intrinsic advantages of that platform: delivering software as a continually-updated service that gets better the more people use it, consuming and remixing data from multiple sources, including individual users, while providing their own data and services in a form that allows remixing by others, creating network effects through an "architecture of participation" and going beyond the page metaphor of web 1.0 to deliver rich user experiences.'[30] Hence, the term web 2.0 describes applications that use the Internet as a technical platform where programs and UGC is provided.[31] The UGC is published by users themselves in contrast to media and brand-generated content, which is provided by the press and companies.[32] In general, the addition 2.0 describes a technical version number, where the number 2 is called release number while the 0 is called level number.[33] According to this, web 2.0 would only describe an extension of web 1.0. Web 1.0 was mostly defined top down, meaning that programmers determined the contents and users could only access them.[34] However, web 2.0 is not only an extension but rather a modified perception of the

27 BVDW 2010, p. 12 (author's translation)
28 As of 18th of November 2012
29 Cf. Huber 2010, p. 14
30 O'Reilly Radar 2005
31 Cf. Alpar et al. 2007, p. 3
32 Cf. Knappe et al. 2007, p. 3
33 Cf. Bastian et al. 2009, p. 79, in: Bastian 2009
34 Cf. Sturm 2010, p. 11f.

Internet.[35] The social aspects of web 2.0 have fundamentally changed the Internet and therefore the rather technical term web 2.0 is not appropriate. The term social web paraphrases its meaning in a better way. Ebersbach et al. understand the social web as one part of web 2.0 that does not deal with technical programs but rather supports social structures and interaction on the Internet.[36] Another term that has arisen within the last years is social media. It is defined by the BVDW as follows: 'Social media is a variety of digital media and technologies that allow users to interact and create media contents alone or together. The interaction comprises the mutual exchange of information, opinions and experiences as well as the contribution of contents. Users actively refer to the contents by means of their comments, ratings and recommendations and hence establish a social relationship. [...] Due to these factors, social media can be distinguished from the traditional mass media [...].'[37] The terms social web and social media hence rather describe the same process while web 2.0 puts the emphasis on technical aspects. Some people agree with O'Reilly's view and associate web 2.0 with technical features while others put the emphasis on the social aspects.[38] Furthermore, there are people who do not see any innovation in web 2.0, e.g. Internet founder Tim Berners-Lee, who states 'If web 2.0 for you is blogs and wikis, then that is people to people. But that was what the web was supposed to be all along'.[39]

Throughout this paper, the term social web will be used to refer to the social part of the Internet. It is described by the author as the **social part of the Internet that enables (personally unknown) people to socially interact with each other**, thereby cherishing old and establishing new relationships. The term social web is not new but was described for the first time already 15 years ago: In 1998 Hoschka used the word social web which would transform the Internet into a social platform.[40] Back then, he predicted the modified Internet. Hence, the social web as we know it today did not come as a surprise but was already foreseen more than a decade ago.

---

35 Cf. Sturm 2010, p. 11f.

36 Cf. Ebersbach et al. 2008, p. 29

37 BVDW 2010, p. 6 (author's translation)

38 Cf. Gehrke et al. 2007, p. 11f., in: Gehrke 2007

39 IBM n.n.

40 Cf. Hoschka 1998

The social web is characterized by three aspects:[41]

- architecture of contribution: due to simple requirements, every user can partake in the social web – even without great expertise
- architecture of networking: on the social web, users upload personal profiles and connect with friends to cherish old friendships and make new acquaintances
- architecture of communication: while formerly only monologues were feasible, the social web enables users to enter into a permanent dialogue.

The social web is enabled and characterized by the following influencing factors:

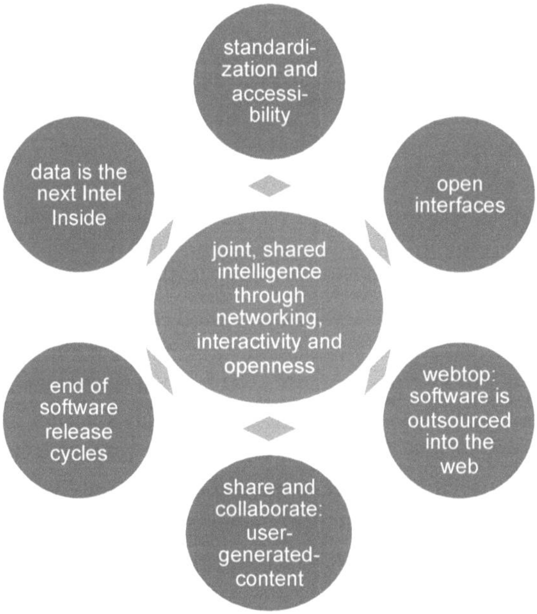

Fig. 2: Components of the Social Web. Source: O'Reilly[42]

41 Cf. Amersdorffer et al. 2010, p. 4f. in: Amersdorffer et al. 2010

42 O'Reilly Verlag 2007, p. 7 (author's translation)

The social web's core – networking and interactivity – is based on many variables. Open interfaces enable users and sites to connect with other users, sites and data. Computer and web applications are merging and more and more software is being completely outsourced to the web. One essential part is the UGC implying that users have the power to determine the social web's content. Furthermore, the classic software cycles ended and applications are continuously refined further online. The social web is not based on programs or technology but on data. Without content the social web would be of no avail. Standardization and easy accessibility enable all users to be an active part of the social web and to interact easily in real-time with one another.[43]

Contents on the social web can be presented in terms of texts, pictures, audio files and videos. Since gestures, mimics and intonation cannot be expressed in written communication, the so-called para-language has evolved in order to deliver emotions.[44]

2.2 Development

Within a short time, the Internet has reached an all-time high: while the radio had to play 38 years and the television had to broadcast at least 13 years to reach 50 million people, the Internet reached this number in only 4 years.[45] From a former technical platform, the Internet has evolved into an advanced living environment.[46] The social web's development was mainly possible due to technical development. In the 1990's, the formerly used modem was largely taken over from the ISDN technology.[47] The speed of loading of today's access is up to 80 times higher than some years ago and the costs of Internet usage have decreased drastically within recent years.[48] In order to publish content, only very little know-how is necessary. Hence, there are practically no entry barriers for active participation in the social web.

The sharing of UGC is enabled by the technologies Ajax (asynchronous java script and XML) and RSS (rich site summary, RDF site summary or really simple

43 Cf. O'Reilly Verlag 2007, p. 7

44 Cf. Kielholz 2008, p. 61

45 Cf. BVDW 2010, p. 13

46 Cf. DIVSI 2012

47 Cf. Bernauer et al. 2011, p. 13

48 Cf. Buss 2009, p. 279

syndication, dependent on the version).[49] Ajax is responsible for the specific data transfer between browser and server; using Ajax, only the new page elements are being uploaded and replaced, making applications much faster.[50] RSS feeds show new content on a site.[51] Users can subscribe to RSS feeds of a certain website and view them whenever it suits them via a so-called feed reader. This represents a great added benefit as users can read all preferred news centrally at when convenient.

In addition to the technical development, there are also economic and social backgrounds for the social web's rapid growth.[52] Economic reasons are the network effect, the long-tail theory and the theory of collective intelligence.[53] The network effect implies that the value of using a network rises with increasing number of participants. Robert Metcalf stated the law that the benefit of a network exponentially increases with growing number of users.[54] This principle can also be applied to the social web: if there are only two members in a community, users can only write to one person. If the community has four members, users can write to three persons and so on. Therefore, the value of the social web as a whole increases with growing user numbers.

The majority of traditional business models focuses on products with a high selling volume. As sales and storage areas are limited, it seems to be economically advisable to concentrate on them.[55] However, due to innovating information technologies these limitations diminish and serving niche markets becomes economically efficient.[56] This effect is described with the so-called long-tail theory, stating that the sum of niche products presents an important market.[57] The long-tail theory is of particular relevance to the social web, where millions of products in terms of pictures, videos, comments etc. are being produced and accessed.[58] It seems that every niche group has their own sites, applications and – most importantly – fans and members.

49 Cf. Back 2009, p. 76f.
50 Cf. Buss 2009, p. 281
51 Cf. Buss 2009, p. 281
52 Cf. Alpar et al. 2007, p. 7f.
53 Cf. Alpar et al. 2007, p. 7f.
54 Cf. O'Reilly Verlag 2007, p. 8
55 Cf. Alpar et al. 2007, p. 8
56 Cf. Alpar et al. 2007, p. 8
57 Cf. Anderson 2008, p. 12
58 Cf. Alpar et al. 2007, p. 9

The theory of collective intelligence states that the collective knowledge of all market players cannot be exceeded by a single market participant.[59] If the knowledge of many is united on the social web, an enormous pool of knowledge is created, surpassing the knowledge of each individual. This can be best illustrated with the online encyclopedia Wikipedia, where every user can publish new articles or modify existing ones. Hence, the extent of Wikipedia is constantly increasing and its content permanently supervised by the crowd. Enabling collective intelligence is seen as the social web's biggest chance.[60]

Social reasons have also favoured the social web's popularity.[61] They can be divided into intrinsic and extrinsic motivators. Intrinsic motivators are caused by the enjoyment of the thing itself and do not depend on an external reward,[62] for example when users have fun publishing holiday reviews and pictures because they somehow experience their holiday once more and want to share their reviews. Extrinsic motivators depend on a gratification, for example when users are active on the social web to make new acquaintances or to benefit in other ways from it. The motivators for the social web usage can be classified into four categories. Although this classification was originally created for the Internet it can be adapted to the social web as well:

59 Cf. Alpar et al. 2007, p. 10

60 Cf. O'Reilly Verlag 2007, p. 8

61 Cf. Alpar et al. 2007, p. 7f.

62 Cf. Kielholz 2008, p. 61f.

identity management	**capital management**	**daily life management**	**emotion management**
autonomy	social capital	daily life structure	sense of community
individuality	maintaining contacts	simplification of daily life	change
independence	extension of contacts	gateway to outside world	relaxation
self-determination	facilitate networking	pastime	excitement
self-realization	cultural capital	flexibility	fun
image	access to world knowledge	reachability	curiosity
anonymity	miscellaneous knowledge		
distinction	competence experience		
legitimacy	economic capital		
group identity	earnings		
	savings (time and money)		
	symbolic capital		

Fig. 3: Motivators for Internet Usage. Source: Pfaff-Rüdiger et al.[63]

According to the classification, there are four different main reasons for being active on the social web. The social web enables users to define and refine their identity. Furthermore, social, cultural and economic capital can be managed. By easily finding like-minded people, it is simple to socialize and to augment the circle of acquaintances. Being present beyond national frontiers, the social web also enables users to interact with other cultures and hence to broaden their horizons. With more and more companies being present, users can also benefit from reduced transaction costs by informing themselves about products and services directly on the social web and in their familiar environment, which saves time.[64] Also, people's daily lives may be improved by the social web since it offers great opportunities for pastime communication as well as the possibility of social interaction 24

63 Pfaff-Rüdiger et al. 2009, p. 53, in: Meyen et al. 2009 (author's translation)

64 Cf. Pfaff-Rüdiger et al. 2009, p. 60f., in: Meyen et al. 2009

hours a day. The social web is also emotionally influencing, for example, when the joint discussion or the sharing of information increase the sense of community.[65]

The social web has already revolutionized today's life. However, the development does not stand still but continues. People are already talking about web 3.0 – the successor to the current social web – which will bring more 3D applications and location-based services.[66] In addition, the semantic web will gain in importance. The semantic web can be defined as an accumulation of information that can be processed not only by users but also by software agents.[67] Moreover, the social customer relationship management will become more important: companies will gain more customer information from the cloud of websites and social web channels. All this information is being evaluated with intelligent mechanisms, allowing companies to provide individually tailored offers to their clients.[68] Although data privacy is a crucial factor, users are willing to exchange personal data for added value and this trend will become even more distinct in the future.[69]

2.3 Usage

2.3.1 User Numbers and Typology

The social web is based on its users, who were chosen as 'Person of the Year' by the TIME Magazine in 2006.[70] Having been passive spectators in the past and having used the Internet only to look for information, users today actively determine the social web's content.[71] They changed from consumers to prosumers[72] and have significantly influenced the social web's development.

The following table presents the changes in the use of the Internet over the last 16 years:[73]

65 Cf. Pfaff-Rüdiger et al. 2009, p. 63, in: Meyen et al. 2009

66 Cf. Ebersbach et al. 2010, p. 272f.

67 Cf. Koch et al. 2009, p. 201

68 Cf. Impulse4Travel 2012, p. 7

69 Cf. Impulse4Travel 2012, p. 7

70 Cf. TIME Magazine 2006

71 Cf. Buss 2009, p. 280

72 Cf. Kagermeier 2011, p. 59, in: Boksberger et al. 2011

73 From 1997 to 2009 the data refer to adults over the age of 14 years in Germany. Since 2010 the Germanspeaking population over the age of 14 years has been surveyed.

	1997	1998	1999	2000	2001	2002	2003	2004	2005	2006	2007	2008	2009	2010	2011	2012
in %	6.5	10.4	17.77	28.6	38.8	44.1	53.5	55.3	57.9	59.5	62.7	65.8	67.1	69.4	73.3	75.9
in m	4.1	6.6	11.2	18.3	24.8	28.3	34.4	35.7	37.5	38.6	40.8	42.7	43.5	49	51.7	53.4
growth in %		61	68	64	36	14	22	4	5	3	6	5	2	13	6	4

Table 1: Internet Usage in Germany from 1997 to 2012 I. Source: ARD/ZDF[74]

74 ARD/ZDF 2012 (a)

Within the last 16 years the German Internet usage has drastically increased. While only 4.1 million people in Germany accessed the Internet in 1997, this number rose to 53.4 million people in 2012. This huge growth was favoured by the new open-mindedness of the population as well as the introduction of easy-to-use, cheaper devices and low-priced access rates.[75] The yearly growth rate has decreased within the last two years, but is still positive. Most of the growth is caused by users over the age of fifty.[76] In 2012, more than 70% of the German population could be reached online. The following table presents the data of Internet usage by gender, age and occupation (occasional usage):

75 Cf. van Eimeren et al. 2012, p. 362

76 Cf. van Eimeren et al. 2012, p. 378

	1997	1998	1999	2000	2001	2002	2003	2004	2005	2006	2007	2008	2009	2010	2011	2012
total	4.1	6.6	11.1	18.3	24.8	28.3	34.4	35.7	37.5	38.6	40.8	42.7	43.5	49	51.7	53.4
gender																
male	3	4.8	7.2	11.1	14.7	16.2	19.2	19.8	20.9	21	21.5	22.7	23.4	26	27	28.1
female	1.1	1.9	3.9	7.1	10.1	12.1	15.1	15.9	16.5	17.7	19.3	20	20.1	22.9	24.7	25.3
age																
14-19 years	0.3	0.7	1.4	2.4	3.3	3.8	5	4.7	4.8	5	4.9	5.1	5	5.5	5.3	5.2
20-29 years	1.3	1.9	2.9	4.6	5.5	6.5	6.2	6.4	6.5	6.8	7.5	7.9	8.1	9.6	9.6	9.7
30-39 years	1.4	2.2	2.9	5	6.1	7.9	8.5	8.9	9.1	8.9	8.5	8.9	8.6	9.6	9.7	9.6
40-49 years	0.7	1.1	2	3.3	5.2	5.2	7.6	7.8	8.1	8.4	8.7	9.4	9.9	11	12.3	12.1
50-59 years	0.3	0.5	1.6	2.2	3.2	3.5	4.7	5.5	5.3	5.6	6.1	6.2	6.6	7.5	7.7	8.7
60 and older	0	0.1	0.3	0.8	1.5	1.4	2.5	2.8	3.7	4.1	5.1	5.1	5.3	5.7	7	8.1
occupation																
trainee	1	1.6	2.4	3.8	5.2	5.5	7.4	6.6	5.5	7.5	7.1	8	7.1	8.1	7.4	7
employed	3	4.6	7.7	12.8	16.1	18.9	21.6	23	24.9	24.2	25.6	26.5	28.4	32.5	32.8	35.6
retiree/ unemployed	0.1	0.4	1	1.6	3.5	3.7	5.3	5.9	7	7	8.1	8.2	8	8.4	11.4	10.8

Table 2: Internet Usage in Germany from 1997 to 2012 II. Source: ARD/ZDF[77]

77 ARD/ZDF 2012 (b)

The table illustrates that there are more male users than female, although the difference between genders has diminished within recent years. In 2012, the biggest online age group was users aged 40 to 49 years, followed by users aged 20 to 29 and 30 to 39 years. There were 8.1 million users in 2012 aged over 60 years. Considering especially the best agers, the trend to an increasing Internet usage within the last years can be observed. While there were only 1.4 million Internet users over the age of 60 in 2002 this number rose to 5.1 million users in 2007 and reached its provisional peak of 8.1 million users in 2012. This number is most likely to grow further as the demographic development increases the number of older onliners.[78] Considering older best agers, every fifth person over the age of 70 is online.[79] This clearly shows that the Internet has become an important medium for all age groups. When searching for information online, best agers remain almost three times longer on the sites when compared to the younger generation as they read the sites' contents more carefully.[80]

Most of the Internet users are employed. The average dwell time per day reached 155 minutes in 2012 and has constantly increased within the last years.[81] In 2012, men spent almost 30 minutes more per day online than women and the age group 14 to 29 years spent the longest time online (168 minutes per day).[82] The most frequently used weekly online activities in 2012 were information seeking on search engines, sending and receiving emails and specific information search.[83] Most of the users surf with a computer, although this number decreased by 18 percentage points from 91% in 2007, to 73% in 2012.[84] Mobile devices gained 16 percentage points in share within the last five years and reached 22% in 2012.[85]

In the European comparison, Germany has a higher-than-average Internet penetration of 75.9% while the European average accounts for only 61%. Only the Scandinavian countries and the Netherlands as well as Great Britain and Switzerland have a higher Internet penetration than Germany.[86]

78 Cf. Janßen et al. 2011, p. 393, in: Thimm 2011
79 Cf. van Eimeren et al. 2012, p. 362
80 Cf. Zangerl et al. 2011, p. 82, in: Law et al. 2011
81 Cf. ARD/ZDF 2012 (c)
82 Cf. ARD/ZDF 2012 (c)
83 Cf. ARD/ZDF 2012 (h)
84 Cf. ARD/ZDF 2012 (d)
85 Cf. ARD/ZDF 2012 (d)
86 Cf. van Eimeren et al. 2012, p. 362

If one classifies the German population, currently accounting to 81.8 million people,[87] according to their online behaviour, the following three groups arise: digital outsiders (40%), digital immigrants (20%) and digital natives (41%).[88] Digital outsiders do not refer to the Internet at all, either because they do not have Internet access and/or the knowledge to go online.[89] Digital immigrants are in the permanent process of learning about the Internet.[90] They appreciate the Internet and use it purposefully on the one hand while they see the connected risks and are skeptic on the other hand.[91] Digital natives were born into the digital world,[92] have grown up with the Internet and have fully integrated it into their daily lives.[93] They are 'native speakers'[94] of the Internet language.

As the general Internet usage has been described in detail, the following paragraphs present the use of the social web. Regarding the social web applications, users state the following usage within the last six years (used at least once a week):

	2007	2008	2009	2010	2011	2012
Wikipedia	20	25	28	31	29	30
video sharing websites	14	21	26	30	31	32
private networks and communities*	6	18	24	34	35	36
media sharing websites, communities	2	4	7	2	3	-
business networks and communities*	4	2	5	5	3	3
blogs	3	2	3	2	1	2
social bookmarking		1	2	1	-	-
virtual games	2	2	-	-	-	-
Twitter	-	-	-	1	-	2

Table 3: Social Web Applications from 2007 to 2012 in %. Source: ARD/ZDF[95]
**network with personal profile*

87 Cf. Weltbevölkerung.de 2012
88 Cf. DIVSI 2012
89 Cf. DIVSI 2012
90 Cf. Prensky 2001, p.2
91 Cf. DIVSI 2012
92 Cf. Prensky 2001, p.1
93 Cf. DIVSI 2012
94 Prensky 2001, p.1
95 ARD/ZDF 2012 (e)

Private networks were the most frequently used social web applications in 2012 with 36% of users accessing them at least once a week, followed by video sharing platforms with 32%. The following table presents the usage of the social web applications by age and gender (used at least once a week):[96]

	men	women	14-19 y.	20-29 y.	30-39 y.	40-49 y.	50-59 y.	60+
Wikipedia	75	70	96	87	78	74	56	49
video sharing websites	65	52	90	85	76	54	39	16
private networks and communities*	43	42	88	74	56	25	23	10
business networks and communities*	9	7	1	14	16	6	4	2
blogs	8	5	12	11	8	4	4	2
Twitter	4	4	5	8	4	3	2	
networks in total	47	44	88	75	61	29	24	11

Table 4: Social Web Applications by Gender and Age in 2012 in %. Source: ARD/ZDF[97]
**network with personal profile*

As the abovementioned table illustrates, men are a little more active on the social web than women. Wikipedia, video sharing platforms, private networks and blogs are mostly used by the age group 14 to 19, followed by the age groups 20 to 29 and 30 to 39. Professional networks are most frequently used by members aged 30 to 39. In Germany, best agers tend to be rather reluctant with regards to social web usage and only 10% are members in a social network. However, looking at the US where 42% of the users aged over 50 were members in social networks in 2012,[98] it is assumable that there is also a trend to an increasing social web usage by German best agers. Currently, the social web is more often used by the younger generation; however, the usage pattern between the age groups may further assimilate in the future.[99]

Regarding the different social web users, the following six social web user types can be identified:

96 ARD/ZDF 2012 (e)

97 ARD/ZDF 2012 (g)

98 Cf. Futurebiz 2010

99 Cf. van Eimeren et al. 2012, p. 364

user type	characteristics
creators	Creators publish content on the social web by writing blogs, posting reviews or uploading photos.
critics	Critics do not publish own content but rather comment on reviews, blogs etc.
collectors	Collectors gather information on the social web with the help of RSS feeds or social bookmarking.
joiners	Joiners are members in social networks.
spectators	Spectators consume content on the social web but do not generate any.
inactives	Inactives do neither actively nor passively consume any content on the social web.

Table 5: Social Web Users Typology. Source: Forrester Research[100]

The social web is based on creators publishing UGC. However, they make up only a small part.[101] Critics do not publish own new content either but refer to reviews by comments. Collectors gather information by using new technologies and joiners are members in a social network. Spectators are an important group because they consume the social web's content. Inactives can be neglected as they do not use the social web at all.

The ratio between the users that actively write articles and those who only passively read them may be explained by the 90-9-1 law by Nielsen:[102] 90% use the Internet solely for information seeking and reading, 9% sometimes publish articles and only 1% write comments and articles on a regular basis. The 90-9-1 law was initially developed for the Internet and not specifically for the social web; however, a similar ratio can be assumed for the social web.[103]

In an international comparison, German users tend to be more passive: US users *share* more content while German users *consume* more content.[104] Since the German social web users are – compared to US users – more consumers than prosumers, new technologies and social web tools can be introduced more easily in the US.[105] As the social web has its roots in the US, the US development is a step ahead, thereby indicating where the German development may lead to. However,

100 Cf. Forrester Research 2007

101 Cf. Forrester Research 2007

102 Cf. Nielsen 2006

103 Cf. Ebersbach et al. 2010, p. 207

104 Cf. Futurebiz 2012 (a)

105 Cf. Futurebiz 2012 (a)

the different usage does not only result from the head start in social web usage but also from different attitudes and cultures. In Germany, privacy and data security is a crucial issue and a decisive condition for German users when publishing personal information is the existence of data security: the willingness to post information increases when the perceived loss of control decreases.[106]

The Internet has developed from a pure information medium into an interactive platform. Besides the vast information possibilities the social web offers, it is also a place of social gathering: as people can meet independent from their domicile, employment and other social factors, the social web presents the perfect place to make new acquaintances and cherish old friendships, since only the common interests are decisive for the interaction. It is predicted that in the future up to 80% of all social contacts will have an online origin.[107]

2.3.2 Mobile Web

The mobile web describes Internet access via mobile devices. It does not necessarily mean using the Internet while being on the move but also accessing it with a mobile device from home.[108] Due to technical developments and decreasing costs, the number of mobile users has steadily increased within the last few years:[109]

106 Cf. Süddeutsche.de 2012

107 Cf. Winter 2007, p. 76, in: Gehrke 2007

108 Cf. van Eimeren et al. 2012, p. 378

109 The data refer to the German-speaking resident population aged 14 years and older.

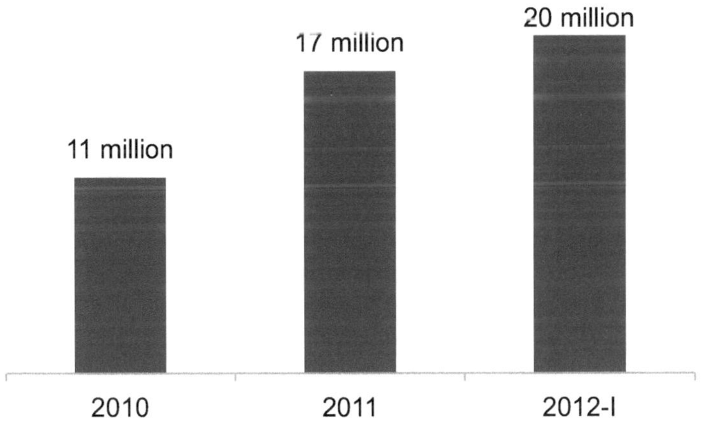

Fig. 4: German Mobile Users from 2010 to 2012 in million. Source: AGOF[110]

While there were 10.95 million mobile users in 2010, this number increased to 16.95 million in 2011 and to 19.8 million in the first half-year of 2012, representing an increase of 80% within only two years.[111] 58.9% of the users are male, while 41.1% are female; the majority of mobile users (68.4%) is aged between 20 and 49.[112] Two thirds are employed and over 40% have a net household income of more than 3,000 € monthly.[113]

The most often used device for the mobile Internet usage in 2012 were smartphones with 84% (out of these, 35% surfed with an Apple iPhone), followed by laptops with 16%, regular cell phones with 5% and tablets with 6% (multiple responses possible).[114] The weekly used applications of the mobile Internet devices are diverse:

110 AGOF 2012, p. 15

111 Cf. AGOF 2012, p. 15

112 Cf. AGOF 2012, p. 18

113 Cf. AGOF 2012, p. 21

114 Cf. ARD/ZDF 2012 (f)

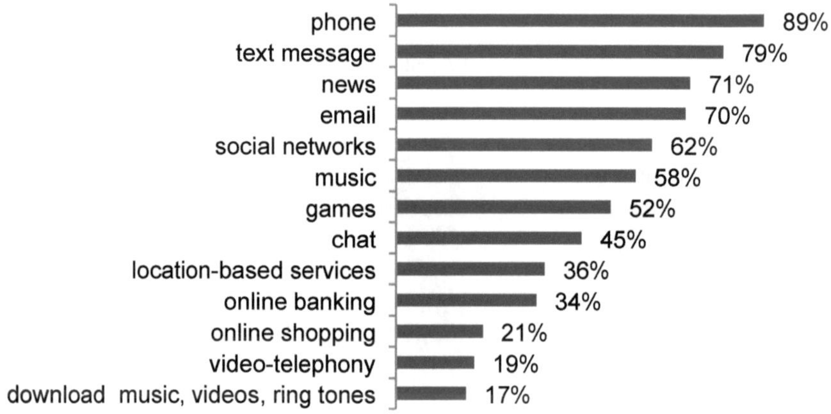

Fig. 5: Applications of Mobile Internet Device. Source: AGOF[115]

While phoning is by far the most used application, at least 21.3% already shop online with their mobile device at least once a week. The mobile users' shopping interests are diverse, as the following diagram illustrates:

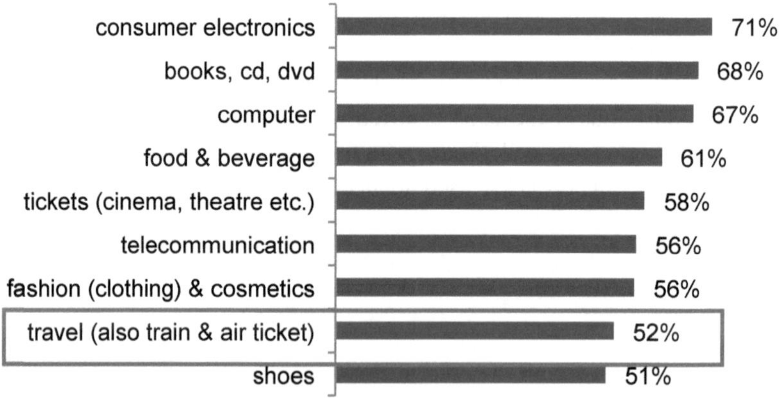

Fig. 6: Top 10 Mobile Shopping Interests. Source: AGOF[116]

115 AGOF 2012, p. 24

116 AGOF 2012, p. 25

Over 50% of mobile users are interested in travel. The mobile web therefore plays a significant role for the travel industry and it is forecasted to soon be a main communication channel for e-tourism.[117] It is also an important travel companion, as the following diagram depicts:

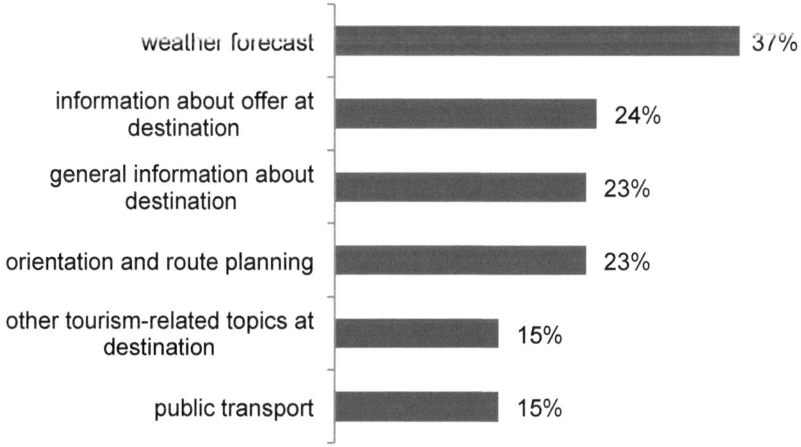

Fig. 7: Mobile Internet Usage on Holidays. Source: VIR[118]

The most important information during holidays, accessed via a mobile device, is the weather forecast. Information about offers at the destination, the destination itself and orientation are further frequent objects of information.

A new technology enabled by the mobile web is location-based services. GPS apps and applications define the users' global position and provide them with information about their current location. As the mobile web will become more and more common, location-based services will gain increased importance, also and maybe especially for the travel industry.

Many companies have already reacted to the increasing use of the mobile web. In addition to implementing a mobile website, more and more companies are taking out ads on mobile devices. However, the success of mobile ads is questionable. 40% of all mobile ad clicks in 2012 were useless with a conversion rate lower than 0.1%.[119] Smartphone users generally click on ads more often than desktop users

117 Cf. Lassnig 2010, p. 15, in: Lassnig et al. 2010

118 VIR 2012, p. 46

119 Cf. Internet World Business 2012

but this may be attributable to the smaller display: every fourth useless click in 2012 was made by accident and 18% of all ad clicks were caused by click cheater programs.[120]

Nevertheless, the mobile web is acknowledged as an important factor and 54% of German hotels state that they plan to communicate with travellers via mobile devices in the future.[121]

2.4 Social Web Applications

The BVDW classifies social web applications into the following four groups:[122]

- group of communication including blogs, microblogs, social networks, podcasts and newsgroups
- group of collaboration including wikis, social bookmarking services and social news
- group of multimedia including media sharing platforms
- group of entertainment including virtual worlds and online games.

In the following, the abovementioned applications are presented and elaborated upon.

Blogs are considered to be the social web's origin.[123] Most often, blogs serve as online diaries where users write articles about chosen topics and upload photos and/or videos. Since personal experiences and opinions are published, blogs are considered subjective in character.[124] Blogs can be protected with a password, so that only selected users can access the content. Because readers can comment on the articles, blogs provide multidirectional communication possibilities. Due to the fact that the number of blogs is constantly increasing, special search engines for blogs were developed. **Microblogs** are shortened versions of blogs and the most popular microblog is Twitter, which is presented in more detail later in this chapter.

120 Cf. Internet World Business 2012

121 Cf. TripAdvisor 2012, p. 5

122 Cf. BVDW 2010, p. 8

123 Cf. Huber 2010, p. 31

124 Cf. Buss 2009, S. 282ff.

According to Tim O'Reilly, **feeds** are one of the most important achievements of the Internet.[125] Feeds can be described as delivery services for online content.[126] Users do not have to look for information actively because they are provided with it: users define topics of interests and so-called newsreaders deliver the desired information via so-called feedreaders.

The term **podcast** is derived from the Apple product iPod and the word broadcasting.[127] Podcasts are audio files which are uploaded and distributed online. Like blogs, podcasts can be subscribed to by users.

Social networks are applications that serve the purpose of online cultivation of social contacts.[128] One can subdivide them into three types of social networks: individual-related, topic-related and mixed networks.[129] Furthermore, they can be classified as open and closed networks. While open networks are accessible for all users, closed networks can only be accessed by a certain type of user, e.g. employees of a company.[130] The average user is a member in two social networks, connected with more than 50 friends and at least 64% access their profile on a daily basis.[131] Social networks have a high viral reach.[132] The most popular social network is Facebook, which is presented in a later part of this chapter.

Newsgroups and fora serve the exchange of questions and opinions.[133] Users can publish and discuss their issues with other users and can hence exchange their views and experiences. Review sites are an especially important form of newsgroups. They can be seen as having an advisory role created by users. On review portals, users publish their product and service experience. Although all experiences have a subjective character and hence may not reflect reality, the average bias is mostly reliable. This fact is also referred to as recommendation consistency.[134] With the emergence of review sites, users no longer depend on the information published by companies but can gain additional, valuable and mostly trustworthy information via the personal experiences of other users.

---

125 Cf. Simons 2011, p. 19

126 Cf. Simons 2011, p. 19

127 Cf. Huber 2010, p. 45

128 Cf. Huber 2010, p. 65

129 Cf. Winter 2007, p. 83f., in: Gehrke 2007

130 Cf. Back 2009, p. 71f.

131 Cf. eCircle 2010 p. 13

132 Cf. eCircle 2010, p. 3

133 Cf. BVDW 2010, p. 9

134 Cf. Mendes-Filho 2010, p. 463, in: Gretzel et al. 2010

The word **wiki** is Hawaiian and means fast.[135] Wikis are a collection of open information that can be viewed and revised by all users. Hyperlinks connect the articles with each other.[136] The most popular wiki is the online encyclopedia Wikipedia.

With **social bookmarkings** a list of the most-popular Internet sites may be created. If users visit a website on a regular basis they can bookmark this site, so they do not have to enter the whole URL again the next time. While these bookmarkings were previously saved within the user's individual browser, they are now set online and can be accessed from any computer and shared with others.[137] The bookmarkings can be associated to different categories and keywords and can be found via a search mask.[138] A popular example is the German social bookmarking service Mister Wong.

On **social news sites,** users rate and comment on news. The news can be provided with a bookmark so it can be found more easily by others. An example is Digg.[139]

On **media sharing platforms,** users can upload photos and videos and make them accessible to others, who can comment on and discuss the uploaded files. The photos and videos are tagged with title and keywords and can be found via a search mask.[140] In addition to a high entertainment value, media sharing platforms also have a high information value because products are not only described in words but also visually shown. The most popular media sharing platform is YouTube.

In virtual worlds, users can create so-called avatars that live in a simulated online world.[141] As an example Second Life can be mentioned, a famous virtual world where companies also participate. **Online games** enable people to play with or against each other despite geographical distances.[142]

As can be concluded from the presentation of the different types of applications, there is an endless number of social web sites and applications, which is

135 Cf. Huber 2010, p. 87
136 Cf. Huber 2010, p. 86f.
137 Cf. Huber 2010, p. 285
138 Cf. Sturm 2010, p. 39f.
139 Cf. BVDW 2010, p. 10
140 Cf. Huber 2010, p. 284
141 Cf. BVDW 2010, p. 10
142 Cf. BVDW 2010, p. 11

continuously increasing. The great variety of social web applications can be illustrated with the following picture:

Fig. 8: Social Web Landscape. Source: FredCavazza.net[143]

As the diagram shows the social web landscape is diverse and sophisticated.

2.5 Social Web and Tourism Industry

2.5.1 The Importance of the Social Web for the Tourism Industry

Tourism has always been considered a very complex, dynamic and information-intense business.[144] In contrast to many other consumer products, tourist services have special characteristics. They are immaterial, non-storable, non-transportable and always include the integration of the external factor: the tourist or guest.[145] For the guests, however, the most important characteristic is that the services cannot

143 FredCavazza.net n.n.

144 Cf. Egger et al. 2010, p. 19, in: Lassnig et al. 2010

145 Cf. Meffert 2000, p. 1160

be tested in advance. As tourist services are complex and carry a high risk,[146] trust plays a major role.

The social web offers vast possibilities for information gathering of tourist services. The social web is applicable to both standardized products like flights and once-in-a-lifetime products like pilgrimages. A hotel overnight stay is a service in between. There are guests who are loyal to a certain hotel group and always stay in its hotels, so-called regular guests. Additionally, there are also guests who have other criteria besides the brand to be met and therefore may frequently change the hotels, so-called new guests. On the social web, both target groups – new and regular guests – may be reached.

Hotels have acknowledged the many opportunities the social web offers. Lots of them are already actively participating and integrating the social web into their marketing activities. They have fan pages on Facebook, send regular tweets[147] via Twitter and write their own blogs, for example. All these measures aim to enter into a direct dialogue with their guests, get informed about their desires and build relationships. The social web may not only be used as a communication platform but also as a distribution channel. Some hotels have implemented a booking widget on their Facebook site, where the booking of the hotel room and further services can be made directly on Facebook.[148] The price may also be influenced by the social web. As an example ITS, a German tour operator, can be mentioned. ITS initiated Facebook bookings in 2012: when booking their holiday via the ITS Facebook fan page travellers receive discounts. The more fans that book the suggested offers, the cheaper the vacation package gets. In the end all travellers pay the same price and, furthermore, travel altogether – so they can make holiday acquaintances even before the vacation begins.[149]

The sale of holidays is predominantly ruled by hard factors like the destination or room amenities.[150] However, it is mostly the soft factors – the people at site – that cause real holiday experience.[151] With the social web, it is easier to get and remain in touch with the local community and holiday acquaintances.[152] Addition-

146 Cf. Egger et al. 2010, p. 22, in: Lassnig et al. 2010

147 A message sent via Twitter is referred to as tweet.

148 An exemplary booking widget can be found in the appendix.

149 Cf. Facebook 2012

150 Cf. Impulse4Travel 2012, p. 4

151 Cf. Impulse4Travel 2012, p. 4

152 Cf. Impulse4Travel 2012, p. 5

ally, users have the chance to plan their holidays together – even with different homes.[153]

Taking all these aspects into account, it becomes apparent that the social web has the *potential* to fundamentally change the way of communication, distribution and also pricing policy of tourist companies. The following subchapters will present the tourist development of the social web as well as tourist social web applications in order to judge the possible impacts of the social web on the tourism industry in more detail.

153 Cf. Impulse4Travel 2012, p. 5

2.5.2 *The Tourist Development of the Social Web*

The tourist development of the social web can be chronologically presented as follows:

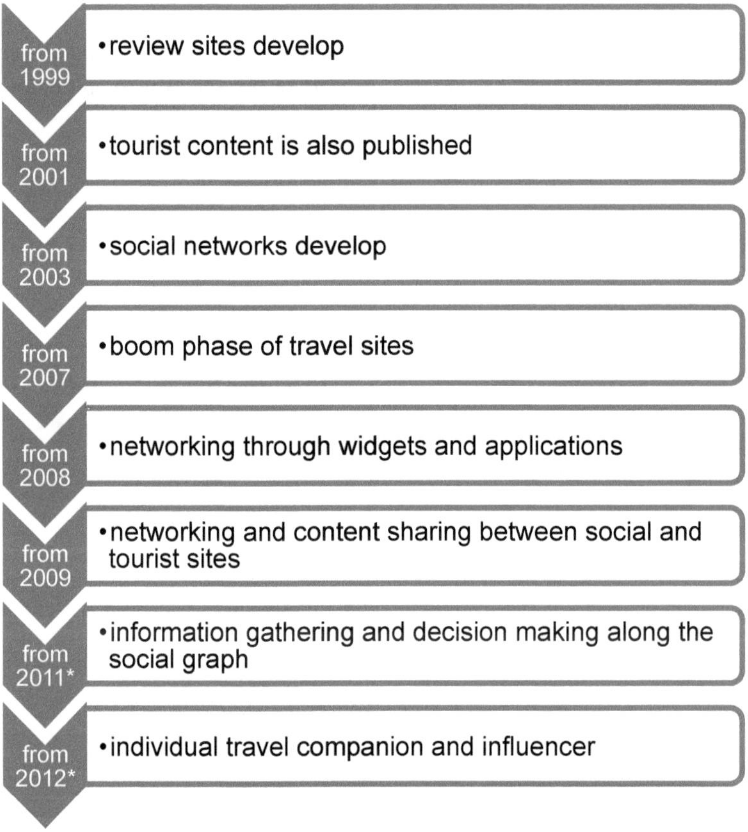

Fig. 9: Social Web Tourist Development. Source: Amersdorffer et al.[154]*. *prediction in 2010*

The beginning of the social web dates back to the year 1999. However, tourist content is not provided until 2001. In 2003, social networks develop and in 2007, travel sites enter a boom phase. The integration of external content on tourist web-sites is enabled by widgets and applications in 2008, resulting in faster content

154 Cf. Amersdorffer et al. 2010, p. 8f., in: Amersdorffer et al. 2010

distribution. In 2009, social and tourist websites are connected, for example, by means of the 'I like' Facebook button on tourist sites.[155] From 2011 onwards, information gathering and decision-making is being made along the so-called social graph. The social graph is made up by the entity of the users' relations and contacts.[156] From 2012, the social web has become an individual travel companion and influencer.[157]

2.5.3 Important Tourist Social Web Sites

According to the Hotelverband Deutschland e.V. (IHA), Facebook, Twitter and Xing are important social web sites for the hotel industry.[158] The importance of the business network Xing is not considered in this paper,[159] however, tourist review sites like TripAdvisor are being added. The following subchapters will shortly present these sites.

2.5.3.1 Hotel Review Sites

On hotel review sites, users share their hotel (and to some extent also restaurant) experiences. They may rate their hotel stay on a point scale or with a written review as well as upload photos and videos. Due to the fact that the content is published, other users can search for specific hotel reviews via a search mask. The reviews are evaluated and a so-called hotel popularity index is often generated, ranking the hotels within a certain area.[160] In Germany the most popular hotel review sites are HolidayCheck and TripAdvisor. Initially developed as pure review sites, today also hotel booking possibilities (sometimes even for trains and flights) are included.

The great majority of hotel reviews is positive: the average review on a scale from 1 (negative) to 5 (positive) reaches the value of 4.3.[161] 80% of all users write

155 Cf. Amersdorffer et al. 2010, p. 8f., in: Amersdorffer et al. 2010

156 Cf. Amersdorffer et al. 2010, p. 386

157 The forecasts for 2011 and 2012 were predicted in 2010, however, the prognoses actually have proved to be true. Today, the social web is a travel companion and influencer and many users communicate during their vacation via the social web.

158 Cf. IHA 2011, p. 166f.

159 The business network XING is understood as a platform where business contacts are being cherished and made. As the focus of the paper is not the impact of the social web on the B2B communication, the business network XING is not taken into account.

160 Cf. Marchiori et al. 2011, p. 103, in: Law et al. 2011

161 Cf. IHA 2011, p. 171

reviews in order to praise the hotel and 90% to provide others with information.[162] The willingness to write reviews has increased significantly within the last two years: while hotels in Frankfurt/Main were evaluated 49 times per year on average in 2009, there were 279 reviews in 2010.[163]

Most review sites offer hotels the possibility to comment on reviews directly, thereby enabling hotels to either thank for positive or react to negative comments. In the real world, a satisfied guest shares his experiences with three, an unsatisfied guest with eleven people.[164] However, this distribution does not count for the social web, where the reviews can be accessed by all users.

The reviews are not only displayed on the review site itself but can also be implemented within third-party sites via widgets,[165] highly increasing the coverage of the reviews. In addition to the 50 million registered TripAdvisor members, another 150 million users read the reviews on partner sites.[166]

Although hoteliers most certainly hope for good reviews, negative reviews are also useful as they create trust.[167] Without any negative evaluation positive reviews seem to be questionable. A study showed that 95% of the users suspect censorship if only positive reviews are available.[168] Furthermore, there are users who purposefully search for criticism. In addition, negative reviews reveal important information about the customers' experiences and opinions. They may help to improve the quality of services. If the hotel reacts properly to complaints, it may appease the disappointed customer. In addition to the real customer reviews, there are also fake reviews, which are published by the hotels themselves or by competitors.

The increasing popularity of hotel review sites like TripAdvisor can be boosted with Google trends evaluations. Since 2004, the Google search volume for TripAdvisor has steadily increased.[169]

2.5.3.2 Twitter

The microblogging service Twitter was founded in 2006. Every member can send shortened messages to the friends (so-called followers). It is a microblogging ser-

162 Cf. IHA 2011, p. 171

163 Cf. IHA 2011, p. 181

164 Cf. Kotler et al. 2007 (b), p. 342

165 An exemplary widget can be found in the appendix.

166 Cf. Tnooz.com 2011

167 Cf. Absatzwirtschaft.de 2012 (a)

168 Cf. Reevo 2012

169 Cf. Google Trends 2012

vice because each tweet may contain only 140 characters. Tweets can be sent and received via different media, e.g. email, sms or special Twitter phone applications.[170] Twitter allows users to interact with each other permanently. Since received tweets can be easily forwarded to personal followers, tweets on Twitter may have a very high outreach. There are currently more than 100 million registered Twitter members worldwide.[171]

2.5.3.3 Facebook

Facebook is a social network, founded in 2004 by the then Harvard student Marc Zuckerberg. Worldwide, Facebook has over 600 million members, 20 million of them residing in Germany.[172] It is a popular social network where users spent around 11% of their online time in 2011.[173] Users create personal profiles, upload photos and videos, write emails, play games etc. All activities are registered and – according to the personal settings – shared with the users' friends. With the so-called 'I like' and 'share' buttons, users can share posts with their friends, thereby highly increasing the outreach.

Facebook was initially developed for private use but has become popular among companies as well. Bauhuber[174] even describes it as the most important social network for the tourism industry. On Facebook, companies can create fan pages and get in contact with users to acquire new guests and to care about existing customer relationships. In addition, Facebook can be used to provide users with information about their products and services. In a survey, 31% of Facebook users stated that they search for products and company information on Facebook, implying a great potential.[175] In contrast to the survey's findings, only 15% of all Facebook and Twitter users are fans and followers.[176] If users become fans, over 50% do so because they want to be informed about the company and its products and want to enter into a dialogue; 40% want to express their loyalty and 26% want to give feedback.[177]

On Facebook, companies can also place advertisements. In addition to standardized banners, it has also become possible to place personalized ads since Au-

170 Cf. Sturm 2010, p. 34

171 Cf. Elcario.de 2010

172 Cf. FAZ.net 2011 (a)

173 Cf. FAZ.net 2011 (b)

174 Cf. allfacebook.de 2010

175 Cf. eCircle 2010, p. 2

176 Cf. eCircle 2010, p. 19

177 Cf. eCircle 2010, p. 18

gust 2012. In order to do so, companies provide Facebook with the email addresses and telephone numbers of their clients which Facebook then imports to its own data base for a data synchronization. All Facebook users who are also customers of the corresponding company may then be provided with specific ad banners.[178] From a data security point of view, this procedure is highly critical.

Although Facebook undoubtedly has developed into an integrated part of the social web, there are critics who forecast that the social network will disappear in the long term. Main points of criticism are the possibility of manipulation, data security, failed flotation in May 2012 and future competition by other providers.[179]

2.5.3.4 Further Social Web Sites

Although the variety of social web sites is already very diverse, new sites are developed continuously.

An interesting tourist social web site is the travel site Gtrot. On Gtrot, friends can connect with each other to discuss their travel experiences, share their future travel plans as well as book future holidays together.[180]

Another noteworthy application is placeme that determines the whereabouts of its users via GPS and automatically calculates how long the users stayed there.[181]

The location-based community WAYN (Where Are You Now?) informs users of all friends within their current vicinity.[182] With WAYN, users can meet friends during their holidays without the prior information that their friends will be in the same destination.

The new social network Google+ was launched in 2011 and is seen as the main competitor of Facebook.[183] It will be only a question of time until tourism providers will be as present on Google+ as they are currently on Facebook.

178 Cf. Focus online 2012

179 Cf. Social Media Akademie 2012

180 Cf. Tourismuszukunft 2011

181 Cf. Futurebiz 2012 (a)

182 Cf. Lassnig 2010, p. 14, in: Lassnig et al. 2010

183 Cf. Focus online 2011

2.6 Corporate Use of the Social Web

2.6.1 Current Social Web Usage

As the social web allows direct dialogues with customers, more and more companies integrate it into their communication concept.[184] It has been acknowledged as an important possibility to reach consumers online[185] and is considered to be fundamental.[186] The classification of a company's communication strategy including the social web can be presented as follows:

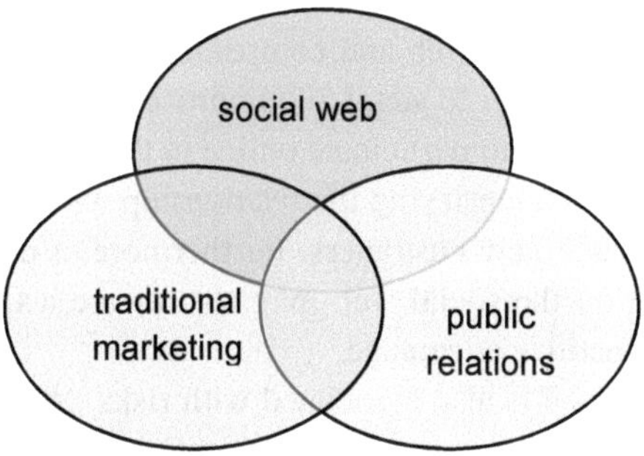

Fig. 10: The Social Web as Part of the Corporate Communication Strategy. Source: Alterian.de[187]

The social web should not be seen as an independent part but rather as an addition to the existing communication strategy by which corporate business models, marketing and distribution activities can be positively influenced.[188]

The company's activities on the social web provide it with a number of unparalleled and excellent opportunities:[189]

- customer retention
- customer relationship management
- innovative product development
- support during customer decision process
- customer acquisition

184 Cf. Hartmann et al. 2011, p. 81, in: Boksberger et al. 2011

185 Cf. Xiang 2011, p. 343, in: Law et al. 2011

186 Cf. Absatzwirtschaft.de 2011

187 Alterian.de 2010, p. 6 (author's translation)

188 Cf. Gehrke et al 2007, p. 27, in: Gehrke 2007

189 Cf. Knappe et al. 2007, p. 72f.

- competitive advantage and strengthening of the unique selling proposition (USP).

On the social web, companies have the possibility to communicate with their customers regardless of geographic distance. Customers on the other hand, do not only talk about companies but also with them thereby enabling a direct dialogue.[190] Customers may be part of the corporate communication strategy,[191] which is becoming faster and more authentic.[192] This enables companies to learn about their clients' wishes in a faster and more direct way: users reveal a lot of information about themselves on the social web and companies can use this information for efficient data gathering in order to adapt and improve their products and services. In fact, every fifth user wants to participate online in the product development of a company.[193] In addition to intensifying the relationship with their existing clients, companies can also reach new customers. Furthermore, a diverse and sophisticated communication on the social web may also create a USP, hence offering possibilities for a competitive advantage.

However, the social web is also associated with risks. Negative reviews are as equally spread as positive and once reviews are online, companies cannot control them. Any published review will remain within the sphere of the Internet.[194] One new phenomenon in this context is the so-called shitstorm. A shitstorm is initiated by users addressing companies with plenty of criticism on social web sites, harming their reputation and brands.[195] Many companies are ill-prepared for them.[196] As users tend to believe the personal experience of others more than the information published by the companies and organisations,[197] the power of word-of-mouth is gaining in importance.[198] As users are becoming more and more informed, they are now able to review the official information published by the companies as well as spread information themselves, of which the company has no influence.[199]

190 Cf. Fabian 2011, p. 6

191 Cf. Kielholz 2008, p. 69

192 Cf. Fabian 2011, p. 6

193 Cf. Bitcom 2010, p. 2

194 Cf. BVDW 2010, p. 15

195 Cf. Absatzwirtschaft.de 2012 (b)

196 Cf. Absatzwirtschaft.de 2012 (b)

197 Cf. Kagermeier 2011, p. 77, in: Boksberger et al. 2011

198 Cf. Hartmann 2011, p. 80, in: Boksberger et al. 2011

199 Cf. Fabian 2011, p. 7

While the external corporate communication was previously reserved for PR and marketing employees, today all employees have the possibility to write about their company, independent of their job position. Although many companies prohibit their staff from writing negative comments by setting out social web guidelines, it can never be completely prevented, especially with former employees. Of course, there are also satisfied employees who are active on the social web who support a positive corporate image.[200]

It is also important to point out that the social web may have a positive impact on the listing on search engines. As search engines are also used during the tourist information process, they have developed into an integrated part of the online marketing strategy for tourist companies.[201] The better the ranking of the companies, the more easily consumers may find them. The ranking of the results of the search engine is calculated according to the relevance.[202] Decisive for the relevance is – amongst other criteria – the currentness of a website, meaning the frequency of content changing. Being based on UGC, social web sites are very current thereby positively influencing the listing.[203]

For many companies, the social web has developed into a central part of the sales and marketing tools.[204] In the following, some studies are presented, analyzing the social web's corporate degree of application.

According to a survey questioning corporate communication managers, the social web's biggest opportunity is the fast spread of information, followed by the improvement of service and the intensification of customer loyalty. The loss of control is the biggest risk perceived. Half of the surveyed companies have a social web strategy. However, the necessary know-how and structural requirements are often not available. It is important to mention that although 31% of the participating companies have a Facebook fan page and 20% already integrate Facebook elements on their websites, only 5% of the surveyed companies have their own social web department.[205]

Another study reveals that the companies' social web strategies are not as goal-oriented as they could be: executives of different branches were surveyed and although 50% are already active on the social web, the majority stated that they have

200 Cf. Bernauer et al. 2011, p. 21

201 Cf. Fesenmaier et al. 2010, p. 381f., in: Gretzel et al. 2010

202 Cf. Reisenzahn 2010, p. 35, in: Lassnig et al. 2010

203 Cf. Reisenzahn 2010, p. 36, in: Lassnig et al. 2010

204 Cf. Reisenzahn 2010, p. 29, in: Lassnig et al. 2010

205 Cf. Fink & Fuchs 2010

no social web strategy at all. The main reasons for participation in the social web are the improvement of image, the increase in revenue and the acquisition and intensification of customer relationships. But one of the most important corporate functions, the monitoring of the social web activities, is neglected. The survey shows that only one in three companies is monitoring the content of the social web, in most cases without any professional tools. 81% have monitoring intentions for the future. Only 5% have one full-time employee for their social web activities.[206]

In a European comparison, 41% of German companies participate in the social web whereas the European average amounts to 44%. 70% use sponsored ad banners on the social web and 51% use the social web to place advertisements for new products. The most important reasons for the social web presence are the increase in brand popularity and customer loyalty, as well as the acquisition of new customers.[207]

A study questioning tourist companies specifically reveals that the Facebook fan page is the most often used corporate social web application, with 48% of the companies being already present. Twitter follows next with 33% of the companies already having their own account. A business entry on Google Places has been made by 23%. 19% have their own YouTube channel and a blog is written by 18%. However, the presentation of social web applications on companies' websites could be improved.[208] The study includes an explicit analysis of the spread of the social web in the hotel industry.[209] For this purpose, hotel brands in Germany, Austria and Switzerland were questioned. Out of these, 74.5% have their own Facebook fan page with averagely 6,161 fans or 'I likes'.[210] 52% of the participating hotels have their own Twitter account with averagely 4,345 followers.[211] The majority (52.1%) has an own YouTube channel and 36.1% include social bookmarking services on their websites.[212] Hotels consider travel experiences, company news, special offers and lotteries to be relevant information for their customers. Few of the surveyed tourist companies allocate the human and financial resources necessary for a comprehensive social web presence and only one third raises more than

206 Cf. FTD.de 2011

207 Cf. eCircle 2011, p. 9f.

208 Cf. Faber 2011 (a), p. 23

209 Cf. Faber 2011 (b)

210 Cf. Faber 2011 (b), p. 5f.

211 Cf. Faber 2011 (b), p. 10

212 Cf. Faber 2011 (b), p. 13f.

4 hours of work per week for it.[213] On average, only 8.9% of the online marketing budget is used for the social web; 71% state that they do not have a social web strategy and only 25% monitor the success of their activities.[214]

According to the IHA,[215] 27.8% of all German hotels are already active on the social web for pr and marketing purposes. 78% of these hotels consider Facebook important while 47% consider Twitter important. Hotel video uploads, e.g. on YouTube, are made by 22% and 18% of the hotels taking part in the study have their own blog.[216] This clearly shows that Facebook currently represents the most important social web site for hotels – apart from review sites. Another study also states that one third of German hotels actively use the social web for their marketing activities, with the highest engagement on Facebook and XING while 27% actively use media sharing sites like YouTube.[217]

The TripAdvisor Index forecasts increased social web activities for hotels in the future:

issue	USA	global
expect social media marketing budget to increase in 2012	52%	50%
plan to monitor social media for mentions of the property	80%	76%
plan to respond to guest reviews about their property on TripAdvisor	91%	87%

Table 6: Corporate Social Web Aims for 2012. Source: TripAdvisor[218]

According to the table, 50% of the hotels questioned globally expect an increase in marketing budget for social web activities, which is an indication of the perceived high importance of it. 76% of the hotels plan to monitor their social web activities and 87% plan to respond to guest reviews, which also indicates that the social web will gain in significance. Generally, US hotels are more actively engaged than the global average. As the social web has its roots in the US, it is not surprising that the US development is more advanced than the European average.

213 Cf. Faber 2011 (a), p. 24

214 Cf. Faber 2011 (a), p. 24

215 Cf. IHA 2011

216 Cf. IHA 2011, p. 168

217 Cf. Riegler et al. 2011, p. 110f., in: Boksberger et al. 2011

218 TripAdvisor 2012

The abovementioned studies clearly demonstrate that the social web has found its way into corporate marketing activities. The social web is considered to be important and active participation is widespread. As stated in the reviewed studies, the most frequently mentioned motivators for the participation in the social web are the intensification of customer loyalty and guest acquisition. The studies further reveal that almost half of German companies are active on the social web. The specific study about tourist companies and hotels also shows a strong acceptance of the social web. Apart from review sites, the most often used application is Facebook. However, the general tone is that there is a lack of human and financial resources. The vast majority cannot provide a full-time employee and only in very few cases is a dedicated social web department existent. Furthermore, social web strategies are missing and the monitoring of the activities' performance is highly neglected.

Generally, the analyses suggest that the social web is accepted by companies as an important factor and represents a significant communication and information channel. The further course of this paper will show if it is deemed as equally important by users.

With their social web presences, hotels try to get in contact with their guests and offer information. By providing certain information and neglecting other, hotels already create an information filter. With the corporate activities on the different social web sites hotels try to raise consciousness for their services in the guest's mind and want to induce preferences with the aim to be considered during the next booking decision.

The social web should never be seen as a detached marketing tool but rather as a useful addition to the existing marketing mix. Most certainly, only guests who are active on the social web can be reached via the corporate communication there. For all others, the traditional marketing activities have to be applied. Therefore, the social web will not substitute the traditional marketing activities.

The information search (on the social web) is a process that is mostly undertaken subconsciously. In contrast to, for example, print advertisements with a coupon for a certain offer for example, the companies' activities on the social web are mid- to long-term strategies that cannot be measured by classic key performance indicators such as conversion rates. However, the current neglect of the social web may cause problems in the future.

2.6.2 Social Web Monitoring and Controlling

As the previous subchapter identified a lack of monitoring, the following explanations will highlight this crucial part of the corporate social web activities in order to create an understanding of its importance.

Social Web monitoring describes the observation and analysis of the content of the social web with the aim to determine the users' current opinion about services, products and companies.[219] Monitoring social web activities enables companies to better observe their competitors, understand their customers and get informed about news and trends.[220] The most important operational areas for social web monitoring are:[221]

- pr and issue management: e.g. fast identification of image problems
- search engine optimization: the social web creates backlinks and relevance, both important factors for the ranking in search engines
- marketing and brand management: the social web provides valuable information about the perception of the company's products and services
- market, industry and competitor analyses: companies can identify new trends as well as compare and assess their competitors' products
- customer service: customer needs can be easily identified
- development of new markets: the observation of the topics being discussed on the social web may result in new business ideas
- generation of leads: especially on B2B sites like XING, interested parties can be identified and properly approached by marketing.

The monitoring process begins with the definition of objectives in terms of qualitative and quantitative numbers. These numbers are then measured and show any need for action. Finally, the disruptive factors are improved or eliminated. The monitoring life cycle can be illustrated as follows:

---

219 Cf. Knappe et al. 2007, p. 118

220 Cf. Futurebiz 2012 (b)

221 Cf. Alterian.de 2010, p. 4

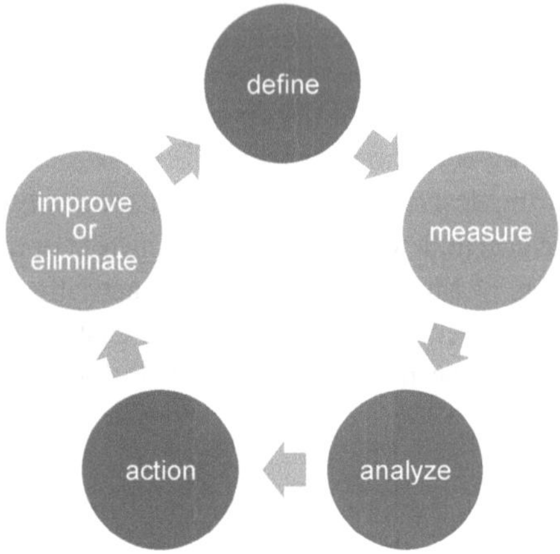

Fig. 11: Monitoring Life Cycle. Source: Alterian.de[222]

In order to keep an overview of all the reviews, comments and discussions that are published on the social web each day, so-called monitoring tools were developed. For hotels, TrustYou is a popular reputation management system. TrustYou aggregates all new content and presents it clearly on one site. Hoteliers can even respond to reviews via TrustYou, eliminating the necessity to search through all of the relevant social web sites.[223]

For a reliable evaluation of the success of social web campaigns, controlling has to be conducted. There is only little information about controlling on the social web due mainly to the fact that not only quantitative but qualitative data also has to be taken into account.[224] However, there are certain success factors that play an important role:[225]

- attention paid to the published content which can be measured by user traffic
- user participation, e.g. comments, reviews and recommendations
- authority of own content, for example the linking from foreign sites to one's own homepage
- influence of the content on users.

222 Alterian.de 2010, p. 8 (author's translation)

223 Cf. Trustyou 2012

224 Cf. Hartmann et al. 2011, p. 84, in: Boksberger et al. 2011

225 Cf. Hartmann et al. 2011, p. 84f., in: Boksberger et al. 2011

A social media scorecard is currently developed by the BVDW to evaluate the success of social web campaigns reliably.[226] This development is a challenging task because metrics of the traditional advertisements cannot be completely adapted to the social web; not only is the number of users important but also the level of engagement, credibility and the dialogue possibilities.[227] Important criteria for the quantitative performance measurement are page impressions, visits, actions, reactions, number of members and coverage.[228] Relevant qualitative factors are activity, relevance, sentiment and commitment.[229] Activity has become an important factor and shows the action of users, fans and followers. Activity can be measured quantitatively by the number of actions (e.g. comments, retweets and reviews) and qualitatively by the coverage, time of reaction and interaction in dialogues.[230] Relevance is also an important factor and describes the importance of and the identification with a topic.[231] The most difficult quality factor to measure is sentiment. It is a rudimentary measurement in the emotionally, socially and digitally networked world.[232] In general, sentiment can be categorized according to three categories: positive, negative and neutral.[233] However, semantic monitoring tools have severe difficulties in analyzing irony and ambiguity.[234] Commitment describes the index of the personal proactive involvement and is composed of the three variables activity, relevance and intensity.[235]

Concluding, it can be said that monitoring is an important part when being active on the social web. When companies opt for a social web presence, it is highly recommended that monitoring strategies also be developed in order to be successful in the long term.

226 Cf. BVDW 2010, p. 80
227 Cf. BVDW 2010, p. 81
228 Cf. Knappe et al. 2007, p. 107f.
229 Cf. BVDW 2010, p. 60
230 Cf. BVDW 2010, p. 58
231 Cf. BVDW 2010, p. 58
232 Cf. BVDW 2010, p. 60
233 Cf. BVDW 2010, p. 60
234 Cf. BVDW 2010, p. 60
235 Cf. BVDW 2010, p. 61

2.7 Summary

The Internet has become an integrated part of our daily life. Today, over 70% of the German population can be reached online.[236] Whereas in the Internet's beginnings, mostly younger and middle-aged users were active, in recent years, however, an increase in online usage among best agers was witnessed and is expected to grow further due to the demographic trend.[237]

The number of mobile users has also strongly increased within recent years and shows great potential for further growth. The importance of the mobile web has been acknowledged by hotels and over 50% plan to communicate with their guests via mobile devices.[238]

The social web – having been defined as the part of the Internet where users socially interact with each other – is an essential part of the Internet and enables users to get in contact independently from geographical or cultural boundaries. It is widely used today. Although there are currently more younger social web users than best agers, a look at the US, where the social web has its roots, may indicate that the social web activities of best agers will further increase in the future.[239] The landscape of the social web is diversified and new applications are continuously being developed. The majority of social web users consists of spectators who gather information from the social web but do not generate content themselves.[240]

The tourist social web development started in 2001 with a small time delay compared to the general social web development.[241] As the tourism industry offers services with a high need for information,[242] the social web provides excellent opportunities with social web sites specifically dedicated to tourism. Especially hotel review sites have gained in popularity as they enable hotel guests to evaluate services in advance. It is therefore assumed that reviews on the social web have a severe impact on the personal booking decision. The information for travellers provided by other users on the social web drastically changes the traditional information distribution and favours the so-called customer empowerment. Customer empowerment can be classified into three dimensions: content empower-

236 Cf. ARD/ZDF 2012 (a)

237 Cf. Janßen et al. 2011, p. 391f., in: Thimm 2011

238 Cf. TripAdvisor 2012, p. 5

239 Cf. Futurebiz 2010

240 Cf. Forrester Research 2007

241 Cf. Amersdorffer et al. 2010, p. 8f., in: Amersdorffer et al. 2010

242 Cf. Egger et al. 2010, p. 19, in: Lassnig et al. 2010

ment (considering the content of the information), social empowerment (interaction with people) and process empowerment (considering processes).[243]

In order to communicate with guests, acquire new customers and cherish existing relationships, hotels have become active to show presence on the social web. The current number of German hotels participating in the social web amounts to 30%.[244] Facebook and Twitter were identified as popular social web sites for hotels. All activities have the overall aim to create awareness in order to positively influence guests in their next booking decision. Therefore, the possibility of social bookings – allowing the booking of hotel rooms on the social web – has already been realized by some hotels. Although there are many hotels wanting to participate in the social web, some may not have carefully considered the consequences. As the presented studies showed, there is a corporate lack of strategy, monitoring and financial resp. human resources. Only few companies have a full-time employee responsible for the social web, indicating that the activities are mostly conducted 'in passing'.

However, the social web is not a guarantee for success but has to be carefully applied. A perfunctory participation in the social web must be strongly advised against. Additionally, it has to be acknowledged that the social web does not replace the traditional marketing activities: there is still a great number of traditional hotel guests who cannot be reached on the social web.

Chapter 2 clearly showed that the social web is widely appreciated and accepted. However, the exact role of the social web for the hotel guest's information process has not yet been defined. The next chapter therefore presents relevant information models and recent online studies.

243 Cf. Mendes-Filho et al. 2010, p. 459, in: Gretzel et al. 2010

244 Cf. IHA 2011, p. 168

3 Tourist Information Search

3.1 Definition of Tourist Services

Hotel accommodations are tourist services which are defined by the following characteristics:[245]

- immateriality: tourist services can neither be seen nor experienced before consumption
- abstractness: tourist services consist of the components time, space, person and are therefore always individual
- perishability: tourist services cannot be stored and are time and space dependent
- uno actu-principle: the production and consumption of tourist services take place simultaneously
- consumption at place of service performance: the services cannot be consumed in the tourist's hometown but only at the place of service performance
- integration of an external factor: the tourist is integrated into the production of service
- service package: the journey is made up by many components.

Regarding the information process, the most important characteristic is that travellers have only few possibilities to rate the services' quality before consumption. In order to minimize the risks, travellers need plenty of information in advance. Therefore, experience and trust are of utmost importance.[246] A relevant important source of information are recommendations by family and friends. The impact of the so-called word of mouth (wom) is especially high in the tourism industry due to the intangibility of tourist services.[247] Therefore, the wom, which may be provided personally or in writing,[248] plays an important role during the information process. The wom is often forwarded by so-called opinion leaders, people who have strong influence on the opinion and decision of others. Especially for the information process regarding tourist services, the impact of the opinion leader is very high.[249] According to the following figure, the information of mass media is not directly passed on to the individuals either but through opinion leaders.[250]

245 Cf. Freyer 2006, p. 135

246 Cf. Wöhler 1993, p. 155, in: Hahn et al. 1993

247 Cf. Raab 2012, p. 25

248 Cf. Knappe et al. 2007, p. 24

249 Cf. Höflich 1993, p. 188, in: Hahn et al. 1993

250 Cf. Höflich 1993, p. 184, in: Hahn et al. 1993

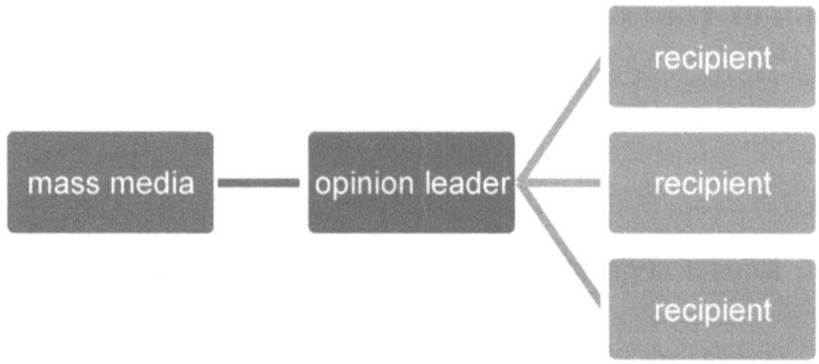

Fig. 12: Two-step Flow of Communication. Source: Höflich[251]

In contrast to the real world where opinion leaders need to have a relation to the recipients, they can be total strangers on the social web.

The information behaviour plays an important role during the buying process regarding tourist services and is one of the most carefully surveyed topics in the tourist marketing literature.[252] However, the majority of the studies deals with information behaviour regarding destination decisions and not the choice of hotels; there is a high need for analyses regarding the information behaviour of hotel guests.[253] In order to develop an understanding for the characteristics of information processes as well as to build a theoretical basis for the later empirical study, the following subchapter will present selected theories.

However, one has to bear in mind that the analysis of the information and buying process is connected with difficulties as the actual decision process is intangible and cannot be observed. The traveller is not always aware of the process either[254] since mostly subconscious activities are influencing factors. A precise definition of the information and buying process is therefore impossible. For the later empirical study this fact implies that it may be difficult to receive clear and distinct results.

251 Höflich 1993, p. 184, in: Hahn et al. 1993 (author's translation)

252 Cf. Egger et al. 2010, p. 19, in: Lassnig et al. 2010

253 Cf. Egger et al. 2010, p. 19, in: Lassnig et al. 2010

254 Cf. Freyer 2006, p. 100

3.2 Information and Buying Theories

Even though tourist buying processes have special characteristics, aspects from general buying theories should also be considered when investigating tourist processes.

The buying process comprises '[...] the whole process from [...] the origin of a certain need [...], via the different types of decision processes including information reception and processing, the selection of a product (purchase intention), the buying behaviour, the use and later disposal of the product to the experience that the customer has gained'.[255] All buying processes are heterogeneous, underlie individual factors and are mostly subconscious.[256] They are influenced by external factors like the macroeconomic situation and culture.[257] Furthermore, they are affected by previous personal experiences, socio-cultural benchmarks, attitudes and habits, emotions and group memberships.[258] The intensity of the information search is dependent on further factors, such as the existing knowledge about the buying objective and the perceived risk.[259] Personal characteristics like age, profession and personality are further important factors for the information and buying process.[260] In this context, Maslow's pyramid of needs should be mentioned which points out that individuals satisfy their needs according to a certain hierarchical order.[261]

Knappe et al.[262] define the dimension of the buying process according to the degree of involvement. The involvement construct derives from advertising research and is seen as one of the most important theories of consumer research.[263] Involvement describes the 'perceived importance of a purchase'.[264] Involvement is highly subjective and has a high influence on the buying process. High-involvement products have a great importance for the buyer, which is why the decision process is very time-consuming. The information sources are specifically chosen

255 Kuß et al. 2000, p. 87 (author's translation)
256 Cf. Kuß et al. 2000, p. 87
257 Cf. Kuß et al. 2008, p. 9f.
258 Cf. Katona 1962, p. 204
259 Cf. Egger et al. 2010, p. 20, in: Lassnig et al. 2010
260 Cf. Kuß et al. 2000, p. 73
261 For further details see Freyer 2006, p. 72f.
262 Cf. Knappe et al. 2007, p. 40f.
263 Cf. Kuß et al. 2008, p. 73
264 Kuß et al. 2008, p. 20 (author's translation)

and the gathered information is thoroughly evaluated.[265] Low-involvement products, on the contrary, are rather unimportant and mostly sources with little information content are being considered.[266] The extent of information processing, reception and the influence of reference groups are dependent on the degree of involvement.[267] Generally, it can be assumed that the higher the involvement, the more complex the buying behaviour.[268] The following table presents the decisive characteristics for high- and low-involvement purchases:

high-involvement purchases	**low-involvement purchases**
comprehensive information processing	learning with repetition of messages
deliberate information search	random information reception
involvement with advertisements	absent-minded reading/listening to advertisements
search for the best/most useful alternative	decision for a satisfying alternative
strong product relation to the consumer's personality, life style etc.	products are unimportant for the personality, life style etc. of the consumer
strong influence of reference group on the buying decision, as the product correlates with norms and values of the group	low influence of reference group on the buying decision, as the product does not correlate with norms and values of the group

Table 7: Comparison of High and Low-involvement Purchases. Source: Kuß et al.[269]

In 1960, Katona[270] defined two types of buying decisions: real (extensive) decisions that are made only occasionally and include the weighing of different alternatives, whereas habitual decisions are being made regularly and out of habit. Extensive buying decisions have a high importance for the buyer and are high-involvement decisions. Besides the financial risk, the wrong decision is also connected with a psychological and social risk.[271] Habitual buying decisions do not require alternatives and little if any information search.[272] They are mostly connected with brand

265 Cf. Kuß et al. 2000, p. 67

266 Cf. Knappe et al. 2007, p. 42

267 Cf. Kuß et al. 2008, p. 77

268 Cf. Kotler et al. 2007 (a), p. 320

269 Kuß et al. 2000, p. 67 (author's translation)

270 Cf. Katona 1962, p. 196f.

271 Cf. Knappe et al. 2007, p. 41

272 Cf. Meffert 2000, p. 102

loyalty and most often the buyer decides for a certain purchase due to previous experiences.[273] Additionally, Katona speaks of impulse buyings,[274] which are described as capricious and incomprehensible. Weinberg,[275] as well, sees impulse decisions as unplanned and uncontrolled. Additionally, there are limited decisions.[276] Due to previous purchase experiences, certain decision criteria arise. The buyer chooses the alternative meeting these criteria.[277] According to these classifications, there are four different buying decisions: extensive, habitual, limited and impulse decisions. However, which type of buying decision is the hotel accommodation? An overnight stay in a hotel may be an impulse decision, for example, when the guest spontaneously decides to spend a night in a foreign city. However, this is an exception as the decision for the stay is mostly made in advance. Most of the time, an overnight stay is not a habitual decision, as guests want to have alternatives and actively search for information. It may only be a habitual decision for very loyal customers who are biased to a certain brand due to positive previous experiences, for example when a satisfied Marriott hotel guest always books a room in a Marriott hotel. This may not be an important exception, however, it is not the general case either. Therefore, the hotel accommodation may not be a habitual decision.[278] An overnight stay may be defined as a limited decision, for example when a regular traveller has already developed certain criteria for hotel accommodation. Only alternatives meeting these criteria are considered. However, since the travel behaviour is a very complex issue, former decision criteria do not necessarily have to apply to future decisions, therefore, the overnight stay is not always a limited decision. Finally, the hotel accommodation is defined as an extensive decision. As the quality of the overnight stay directly impacts on the guests' satisfaction, it is connected with a high degree of involvement. Differences between alternative hotels are perceived and evaluated and apart from regular business travellers, the hotel accommodation is a service that is being requested irregularly. With the exception of last minute bookings, the booking decision is made with a certain lead time and without time pressure. According to Kuß et al., it is an extensive buying decision if all the abovementioned characteristics are met:

273 Cf. Kuß et al. 2000, p. 100

274 Cf. Katona 1962, p. 203

275 Cf. Weinberg 1981, p. 13f.

276 Cf. Weinberg 1981, p. 12

277 Cf. Weinberg 1981, p. 13f.

278 This does not apply to certain business guests where the decision process is mostly determined by external factors, such as special company rates.

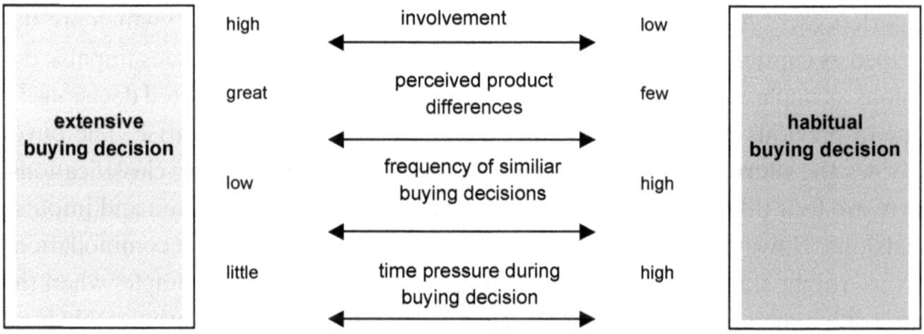

Fig. 13: Extensive and Habitual Buying Decision. Source: Kuß et al.[279]

Hence, the hotel accommodation is generally identified as an extensive buying decision with high involvement.[280] For the information and booking process, this identification entails certain consequences as it becomes more complex and more profound. Most certainly, it should be acknowledged that there are also guests who prefer to book their hotel room out of habit rather than to conduct profound information search. In this case and for those guests, the overnight stay is a low-involvement service. It can therefore be stated that the degree of searching information – also on the social web – is dependent on the degree of personal involvement.

According to Freyer,[281] one can differentiate between three types of decision processes:

- travel decision as a dynamic process: AIDA model
  The AIDA model consists of four phases: the attention and the demand resp. need for holidays is raised by advertisements and media reports for example. If interest aroused, the search process begins. Based on all gathered information the decision is made. The action phase begins with the actual consumption of the tourist services. Knowing about these four phases, external third parties may positively influence the buying decision by specifically providing information.[282]

279 Kuß et al. 2008, p. 115 (author's translation)

280 As depicted, the overnight stay may most certainly also be an impulse, limited or habitual decision, however, it is considered to be an extensive decision for the great majority.

281 Cf. Freyer 2006, p. 104ff.

282 Cf. Freyer 2006, p. 105

- travel decision as a (hierarchical) multi-stage process: similar to the AIDA model there are further studies implying a multi-stage decision process but not with the focus on the time lapse but rather on the complexity and different meaning of the partial decisions. Tourist decisions cause a complex process, consisting of various partial decisions regarding the different components of the holiday. Theoretic models divide the travel decision into a process where complex decision tasks are done in a certain order, which creates different hierarchies of the decisions. This decreases the decision's complexity as the decisions are being made one after the other according to hierarchy.[283]
- behavioural scientific models: the behavioural science is guided by consumer research and explains and forecasts consumer behaviour with the help of theoretical modelling. The approaches can be subdivided into two parts: black box models (s-r-approach) and structural approaches (s-o-r-approach). Black box models define the behaviour as a reaction (r) to an observable stimulus (s). The mental processes during a buying decision are not observable and therefore referred to as black box which is not investigated. The focus of investigation is the reaction on changing influencing factors. Structural approaches focus on the structuring of the black box and investigate the non-observable processes in the organism (o).[284]

This paper takes the view that the buying process is not a single activity but is comprised of certain phases. A popular model for the investigation of these single phases is Kotler's five-phase model,[285] consisting of the following steps:

283 Cf. Freyer 2006, p. 106

284 Cf. Freyer 2006, p. 106f.

285 Kotler's five-phase model is chosen although it is not specifically designed for tourist information processes. It is, however, well applicable to the hotel information process.

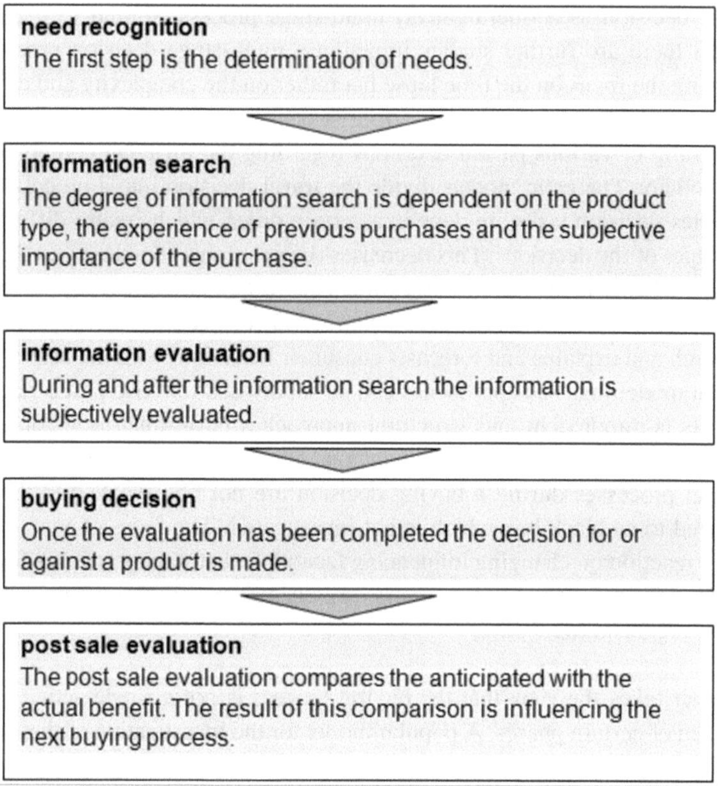

Fig. 14: Kotler's Five-phase Model. Source: Kotler et al.[286]

The following paragraphs will describe each phase with regard to the hotel information process.

need recognition

Need recognition presents the beginning of each buying decision process and arises due to a discrepancy between an actual and a desired situation.[287] There is only little literature about the development of needs.[288] Kotler et al. differenti-

286 Cf. Kotler et al. 2007 (a), p. 295f. (author's translation)

287 Cf. Bänsch 2002, p. 296

288 Cf. Kuß et al. 2000, p. 90

ate between external and internal need triggers.[289] External triggers arise due to external circumstances, for example when a hotel has to be booked for a family reunion. Internal need triggers are being caused by the guests themselves, such as the desire for a wellness trip. Internal needs can also be caused by external factors, e.g. printed advertisements for a nice wellness hotel.

information search

Once the need has been internally consolidated, the consumer starts searching for information. The extent of the information processing and reception is dependent on the level of involvement.[290] As the hotel accommodation has been generally identified as a high-involvement service, it can be assumed that the dimension of the information search is rather high accordingly. During the information search, consumers may use four different sources:[291]

- personal sources (previous stay at the hotel)
- commercial sources (hotel brochure)
- public sources (independent reporting)
- experience sources (experience from friends and family).

The information search primarily takes place in order to reduce the risks involved with the later decision. The hotel guest may be exposed to the following risks:[292]

- functional risk (e.g. overbooking, no hotel room available)
- distress risk (e.g. allergy-sufferer staying in a smoking room)
- financial risk (e.g. room rate paid too high)
- social risk (e.g. hotel is 'not good enough' to be seen in)
- psychological risk (e.g. hotel does not meet personal standards)
- time risk (e.g. information search has to be reactivated because first choice is not available).

289 Cf. Kotler et al. 2007 (a), p. 296
290 Cf. Kuß et al. 2008, p. 77
291 Cf. Kotler et al. 2007 (a), p. 296
292 Cf. Kotler et al. 2007 (a), p. 303

information evaluation

The evaluation of information is a heterogeneous process where all the collected information is being evaluated subjectively. During the evaluation, the information source is also considered. While friends and family provide highly subjective information, hotels may publish only positive information, thereby maybe warping the actual facts. As there is a high credibility of wom for tourist services, the experiences of friends and family are especially important information.[293]

buying decision

After having considered and evaluated all relevant information, the guest finally makes his booking decision and begins with the actual booking process.

post sale evaluation

During the post sale evaluation – after departure – the guest compares his expectations, which were established during the information process, with the actual services experienced. If the expectations are not met, the guest is unsatisfied and will most likely not book a room at the hotel again. If the expectations are met or exceeded, the hotel may be considered during the next booking decision. The experience as a whole adds new criteria for the next personal information process and also to the processes of others if the guest shares his or her experiences, e.g. on review sites or social networks.

The presentation of the theories reveals important aspects for further understanding. The dimension of the buying and information process depends on the level of involvement. Generally, the hotel overnight stay is defined as a high-involvement service and is therefore connected with a complex buying and information behaviour, which is subconsciously influenced and therefore difficult to measure and define. Kotler's model adequately presents the different phases during the information process; they are also valid for a hotel booking. As already mentioned before, the information process is cognitively controlled and includes – in the case of a hotel booking – a high emotional involvement. Therefore, socio-psychological aspects are also influencing factors. This topic cannot be further investigated at this point as it would exceed the scope of this paper, however, it is advised that further empirical studies, dedicated to the socio-psychological aspects, are conducted.

The general theoretical background for the information process has been set. However, as chapter 2 presented, there are profound changes in the usage of the

293 Cf. Wöhler 1993, p. 157, in: Hahn et al. 1993

Internet and the social web. These changes entail that information and buying processes have to be reconsidered.[294]

The following subchapter will investigate how the hotel information process is impacted by the social web.

3.3 Social Tourist Information Search

As the hotel overnight stay is generally a high-involvement service, the information process plays an especially important role. Having divided the hotel information process into several phases, the following paragraphs investigate if and how the social web is an influencing factor.

According to Kotler's model, each buying process begins with *need recognition*, which may be caused by internal and external need triggers. At this point, the social web already plays a crucial role as the social web itself may initiate the need. Users may read positive reviews on TripAdvisor, view holiday pictures on YouTube or read about their friend's holiday experience on Facebook – all these input factors may develop the urge for a holiday or a hotel overnight stay and may create a so-called me-too feeling. Hence, the social web may create awareness and need in the first place. Users are exposed to this information, even if they do not actively search for it. They may be exposed to it simply by being online, for example when a posted holiday picture is shown in the news section on Facebook. Assuming that there is a social response to Kotler's model, it should not begin with *need recognition* but rather with *need generation* as the social web may be a catalyst for the need for holidays. Therefore, a pre-stage should be added to Kotler's model, namely need generation.

The social web offers great opportunities for the hotel *information search.* As already discussed in detail, the UGC provides very valuable information to guests and dramatically changes the power of information.[295] Also, as time has developed into a limited resource[296] users appreciate preconceived opinions, which reduce the time for the information search.[297] Reviews and experiences by others enable guests to evaluate the hotel's services in advance more easily, thereby minimalizing the risk of dissatisfaction. However, the biggest advantage of the social web –

294 Cf. Knappe et al. 2007, p. 39

295 Cf. Knappe et al. 2007, p. 67

296 Cf. Knappe et al. 2007, p. 45

297 Cf. Knappe et al. 2007, p. 62

the great amount of information – also bears risks. Users can only gather a certain amount of information before the so-called information overload occurs, a state of mind in which a person is unable to process any further information.[298]

As described in the previous subchapter, wom plays an essential role in the tourist information process. While the traditional wom only considers personal sources, the electronic wom (ewom) also takes the opinion of other personally unknown people into account. The opinion of each consumer is gaining importance.[299] Ewom '[...] is typically defined as positive or negative statements made by potential, actual or former guests about a product or company available to the public via the Internet'.[300] The credibility of ewom is especially high and crucial for tourist services.[301] In contrast to the traditional wom, ewom has certain advantages, such as lower costs, a broader scope and an increasing anonymity; in addition, ewom can be accessed independently of geographic limitations[302] and is spread faster and more widely.[303] For hotel booking decisions, e-wom in the form of reviews and comments is a very important factor.[304] Ewom is changing the balance of power between hotels and guests, as guests may severely influence the hotel's image through their reviews.[305] Due to the fact that all reviews are based on a personal, subjective point of view, not all of them may be reliable. However, in their totality they should present an overall impression close to reality. These personal experiences may also help to verify the information published by hotels. Consequentially, the *information evaluation* is also influenced positively. A central part of the social web is the possibility to comment on reviews and posts of others directly. If an unjustified complaint is published online, e.g. on TripAdvisor, users – and of course hotels as well – may directly respond and address the matters mentioned appropriately. As explained in the previous subchapter, consumers consider four different types of sources, namely personal, commercial, public and experience sources.[306] On the social web, users may interact with their personal sources, e.g. on social networks. They also get in contact with commercial sources,

298 Cf. Kuß et al. 2000, p. 112

299 Cf. Knappe et al. 2007, p. 57

300 Jiang et al. 2010, p. 299, in: Gretzel et al. 2010

301 Cf. Jiang et al. 2010, p. 300, in: Gretzel et al. 2010

302 Cf. Ip et al. 2010, p. 347, in: Gretzel et al. 2010

303 Cf. Maurer et al. 2011, p. 499, in: Law et al. 2011

304 Cf. Marchiori et al. 2011, p. 103, in: Law et al. 2011

305 Cf. Schegg et al. 2010, p. 437, in: Gretzel et al. 2010

306 Cf. Kotler et al. 2007 (a), p. 296

for example when they like a hotel's Facebook fan page. Public sources may be accessed via Wikis and experience sources on review sites like TripAdvisor. The social web therefore enables users to access the four prevalent information sources but to a much greater extent than offline information could ever provide.

Once information has been gathered and evaluated, users make their *booking decisions*. However, until the booking process is fully completed, there is only a booking intention. In times of the social web, this booking intention cannot only be altered by a change of situation or the influence of friends and families,[307] but also by the influence of other users on the social web. Additionally, the booking itself can also take place directly on the social web, for example with a booking widget on Facebook, thereby influencing not only the information but also the actual booking process.

The *post sale evaluation* is most likely one of the phases impacted the most by the social web. While formerly personal experiences would only be shared with friends and family, today they can be published and made accessible to the whole online world. The published reviews have a very widespread reach as the social web has neither geographical nor demographical limitations. The high scope combined with the high credibility of wom is a crucial factor.[308] In addition to sharing the experiences with others, the social web also enables guests to contact the hotel to post a complaint or an appraisal or simply to stay in touch.

As depicted, the social web has the potential to influence the information and booking process fundamentally. On the social web users are exposed to a great variety of information which may also cause a need for certain products and services in the first place. If the active information search begins however, only a small part of the social web's content is accessed and the search is narrowed down to specific sites and applications. Guests looking for reviews by others visit review sites, users looking for photos search on YouTube and those who would like to get in contact with the hotel directly may go to the hotel's Facebook fan page. The after-sale evaluation also takes place only on certain sites. The phenomenon of considering only a few websites during the information process may also be referred to as the *filtering effect*[309] of the social web.

The AIDA concept, according to which products and services first arouse attention, resulting in interest and decision and finally in a course of action, was

307 Cf. Kotler et al. 2007 (a), p. 302

308 Cf. Knappe et al. 2007, p. 55

309 Author's definition. The study conducted by the Cornell University, which will be presented in chapter 3.4 also shows that the information search is narrowed down to a small number of sites.

presented. This model may also be applied to the social web: the social web's content (unintentionally) creates attention for a hotel. During the information search, interest is awakened, resulting in a decision for the booking and the later course of action that follows when the overnight stay occurs. The post sale evaluation – with reviews being published on social web sites – may then attract the attention of other users, activating the whole process again. Even if the personal review is being published only on one specific site, it is nevertheless pushed out in the great atmosphere of the social web. Due to the fact that one important aspect of the social web is the architecture of networking,[310] it is implied that there is a crosslinking between contents and sites. The aspect of the filtering effect can be graphically combined with the AIDA model:

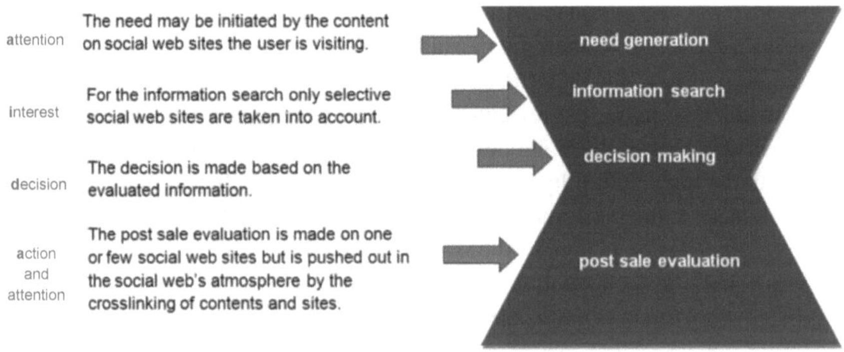

Fig. 15: Filtering Effect of the Social Web. Source: own survey

During the information process, the social web serves as a funnel where the search is narrowed down to specific sites. Simultaneously, the AIDA process takes place.

As depicted, the social web has the *theoretical* chance to greatly impact the whole information process, as it presents numerous possibilities for the information search, the final booking and the post stay evaluation. The next subchapter will present online and social web studies in order to see if and how the information process is also *practically* influenced.

310 Cf. Amersdorffer et al. 2010, p. 4, in: Amersdorffer et al. 2010

3.4 Online and Social Web Studies

There is currently a great hype surrounding the social web and it seems to become an increasingly important part during the tourist information process. This sub-chapter investigates if and how the social web is currently used as an information source to analyze its effectiveness. There are various studies about the use of the Internet and the social web regarding holiday preparation. In order to give an overview of the current use, selected studies, first about the Internet in general and then specifically about the social web, will be presented.

As the following figure demonstrates, the Internet has steadily gained in importance for holiday preparation and booking within recent years:

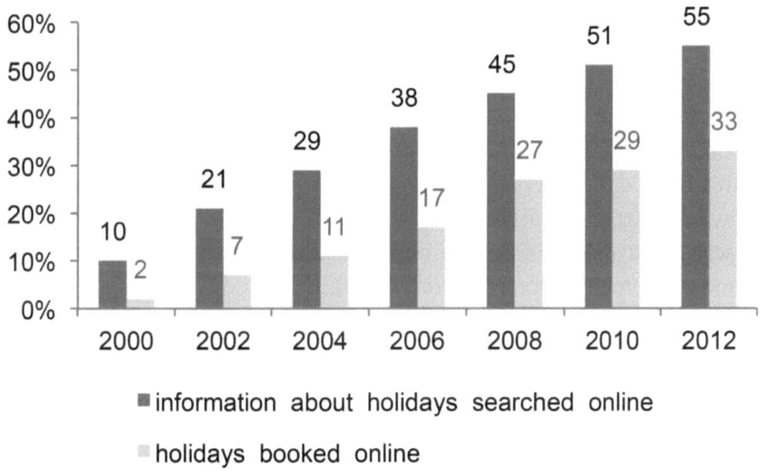

Fig. 16: Internet Usage for Holidays I. Source: *VIR*[311]

While in 2000, only 10% of the German population accessed the Internet for gathering information about holidays, the number climbed to 55% by January 2012.[312] The number of online bookings as well increased during that period, from only 2% in 2000 to 33% in 2012. The most sought-after information concerns destination (31%), price comparison (30%), accommodation (27%) and package and mod-

311 VIR 2012, p. 21

312 German-speaking population aged 14 years and older (until 2010 only Germans).

ule holiday (20%).[313] The most frequently booked online services are accommodations (15%), package and module holidays (9%) and flight tickets (9%) (multiple responses possible).[314] If one classifies the German population according to their online and travel activities, the following numbers arise:

	population	online population	online travellers
	14+ years	**14-70 years**	**14-70 years**
share of population	100%	68%	59%
Internet used for information	55%	77%	84%
Internet used for booking	33%	47%	68%

Table 8: Internet Usage for Information and Booking. Source: VIR[315]

The important target group in terms of online reachability are online travellers, already making up 59% of the German population. Out of all online travellers, 84% have already used the Internet as an information source and 68% already booked a holiday or a part of it online.

Those who have not yet booked online held the lack of contact with a person (32%) and the perceived complication of booking online (20%) responsible.[316] The study shows that when looking online for holiday information, travellers spent an average of 9 hours visiting an average of 13 different websites.[317]

The importance of the Internet as an information medium is also confirmed by another study:[318]

313 Cf. VIR 2012, p. 21

314 Cf. VIR 2012, p. 22

315 VIR 2012, p. 23

316 Cf. VIR 2012, p. 25

317 Cf. VIR 2012, p. 24

318 Cf. ADAC 2011, p. 55

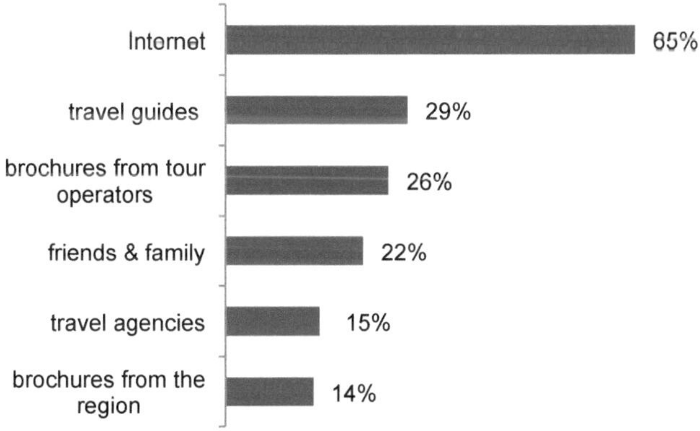

Fig. 17: Internet Usage for Holidays II. Source: ADAC[319]

With 65.1%, the Internet is currently the most significant source of travel information by far. With a large gap travel guides follow with 28.7% and brochures from tour operators with 25.6%. Friends and family are being consulted by 22.2%. The most sought after information concerns accommodation (52.3%).[320] 46.2% of the respondents made a complete or partial holiday online booking in 2010.[321]

In 2010, city travellers in three European cities were questioned about the role of the social web during holiday information gathering. Almost half of the respondents (45.1%) used review sites, 37.1% social networks and 32.1% travel communities during their information process. However, blogs, photo and video sharing platforms as well as microblogs only played a minor role. The three mostly sought information concerned sightseeing (56.4%), accommodation (48.4%) and transport (47.5%) (multiple responses possible). The social web is perceived as a *very important* holiday information source by 21.8% and as an *important* information source by 39% of the respondents. The vast majority however, uses the social web passively, only accessing information but not creating own content. Regarding the different age groups, the study shows that the age of travellers using the social web is on average higher than those not using it.[322] Furthermore, the study presents a correlation between the length of stay and the social web usage: the longer the duration of the stay, the more some travellers use the social web as an informa-

319 ADAC 2011, p. 55

320 Cf. ADAC 2011, p. 53

321 Cf. ADAC 2011, p. 57

322 It has to be mentioned that the study questioned only travellers aged between 14 and 35 years.

tion source. The social web is equally used by first-time and repeat destination travellers, with the exception of review sites which are more frequently used by first-time travellers.[323]

In a conducted study about the importance and credibility of online hotel reviews, 93% of the travellers state to use Internet sites as a decision support before booking a holiday; 96% are influenced by reviews about accommodation.[324] The following diagram gives an overview of the use of booking and review sites:

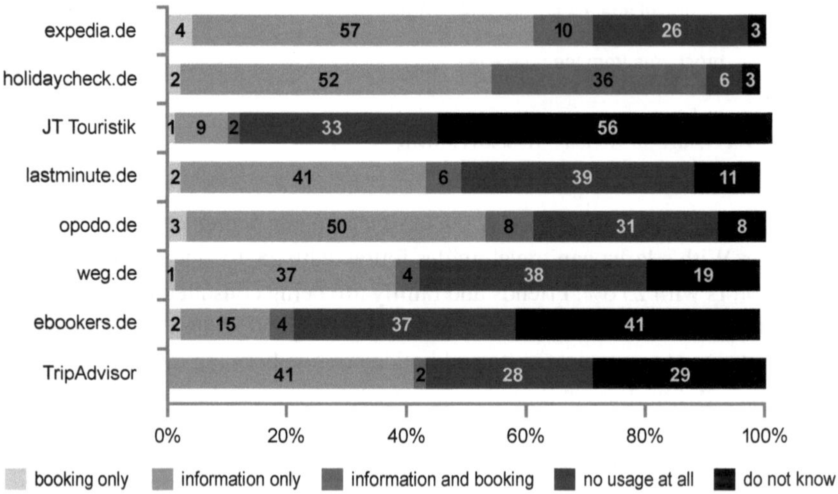

Fig. 18: Use of Hotel Review and Booking Sites. Source: VIR et al.[325]

As the figure shows, the two review sites HolidayCheck and TripAdvisor are considered important information sources: 52% use HolidayCheck as an information source and another 36% access it to gather information *and* make the booking. Only 9% do neither use nor know this site. TripAdvisor is used by 41% as an information source, however only by 2% as an information *and* booking source. 57% do not know or use this site at all. This huge difference between these two similar websites is based on the fact that HolidayCheck is more popular in Germany whereas TripAdvisor is more present on an international level. The surveyed

323 Cf. Raab 2012, p. 150f.

324 Cf. VIR et al. 2011, p. 19f.

325 VIR et al. 2011, p. 21

booking sites with review function are also actively used as an information source, however, the review portal HolidayCheck generates most of the bookings. Indications for reliable reviews are the number of reviews, the quality and detail level of the reviews and the number of photos.[326] Authenticity has the highest influence on credibility and 95% consider reviews on Internet sites to be authentic.[327] 75% of the surveyed guests state that the booked hotel meet the expectations created by reviews.[328] For business travellers, reviews play an important role as well: 58% of business travellers are highly influenced by them.[329]

Regarding the type of used social web sites, the following distribution arises (multiple responses possible):

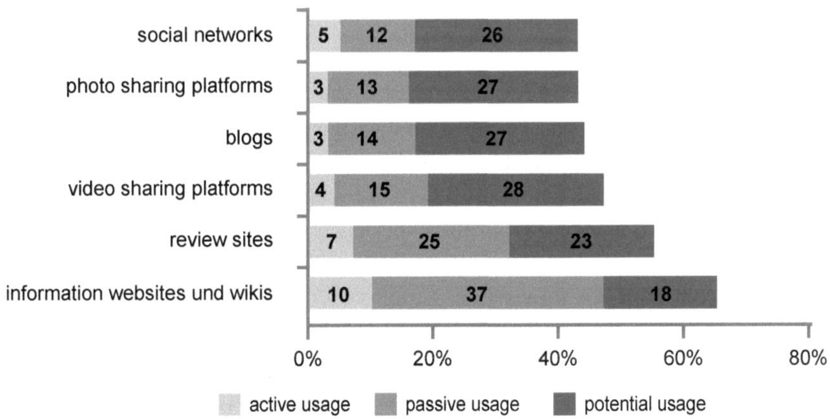

Fig. 19: Social Web Sites Used for Holiday Information Search. Source: VIR[330]

Passive users access the sites to read reviews and comments by others only, while active users also share own experiences. Potential users have not used the sites for holiday information so far, but can imagine doing so in the future. Mostly, the sites are used passively without any active contribution. The most frequented sites are information websites and wikis, followed by review sites. With a certain distance video sharing platforms, blogs, photo sharing platforms and social networks fol-

326 Cf. VIR et al. 2011, p. 23
327 Cf. VIR et al. 2011, p. 23f.
328 Cf. VIR et al. 2011, p. 30f.
329 Cf. VIR et al. 2011, p. 63
330 VIR 2011, p. 35

low. Users aged 50 and older make up 33% of all active users, showing that the older generation also shares UGC.[331]

A study in which US hotel guests were surveyed about their information sources reveals that the most frequently consulted social web sites are the US rating program AAA and TripAdvisor. Third is Facebook with over 10% of the guests using it as an information source. Blogs are used by about 5% of the users, YouTube by around 4% and Twitter by about 3%.[332] While TripAdvisor and blogs are more often used by women, Twitter and YouTube are more frequently consulted by men. Facebook is used by both genders to the same extent. For the majority of all users, the information search begins with a search engine.[333] However, there are significant differences during the early, middle and late stages of information gathering. While many different sources are being used in the first stage, it is narrowed down to certain sites in the late stage.[334] The probability of booking a hotel with negative reviews has decreased to the number of 2 on a scale from 1 (unlikely) to 5 (likely), hence, negative reviews have a strong impact on the booking decision. The same applies to the likelihood of booking a hotel with positive reviews where the average number is 3.5.[335] The readiness of posting a review after the hotel stay is independent from the experience: positive and negative reviews are posted to the same extent.[336] Generally, the study proves a strong acceptance of the social web for US hotel guests.

According to a study investigating the role of the social web in the hotel industry, the booking decision is significantly influenced by review sites. The majority of the guests expects that hotels respond to reviews. However, only 24% of the respondents would become a Facebook fan of the hotel and less than half are interested in direct communication and interaction with the hotels.[337] Only 16% are looking for links to social web sites on the hotel's homepage. In addition, advertisements on Facebook are not perceived positively. According to the study, the potential for social media marketing in the hotel industry is not as high as expected.[338]

---

331 Cf. VIR 2011, p. 35

332 Cf. Cornell University 2010, p. 13

333 Cf. Cornell University 2010, p. 15

334 Cf. Cornell University 2010, p. 15

335 Cf. Cornell University 2010, p. 16

336 Cf. Cornell University 2010, p. 18

337 Cf. iTronix 2011, p. 5

338 Cf. iTronix 2011, p. 5

A study surveying hotel guests upon arrival about their information and booking behaviour reveals that the most used online information sources are the hotel's website (73.5%), booking sites (51.7%) and review portals (40.4%) (multiple responses possible). Review sites are perceived as the most important information source (32.9%). The study shows that almost one fourth of the guests begin their information search with a search engine, switching then to either the hotel website or booking sites. As already mentioned in chapter 2, social web activities may also positively influence the ranking on search engines. The importance of search engines for hotels is undoubtedly confirmed with this study, according to which almost one quarter of the hotel guests start their information process there.[339]

The presented study demonstrated that the Internet plays a crucial role for holiday preparation. It was shown that the social web is also used as a source of information. However, mostly review sites are considered during the information process. The great majority uses the social web passively and do not contribute any content themselves.

3.5 Summary

Chapter 3 defined the hotel accommodation as a high-involvement service with special characteristics. The most important characteristic is that the services can only be evaluated at the time of consumption and not in advance. Due to the fact that the guest is directly affected by the services' quality, reviews and experiences of others during the information gathering are especially important. The (e)wom is seen as a crucial factor during the information process. The information process itself is a complex process which is mostly undertaken subconsciously and therefore difficult to measure.

There are different buying and information theories in consumer and tourism research. Kotler's five-phase model was presented, which divides the information process into five different phases. This model was applied to tourist information processes and it was proven that it is highly impacted by the social web. It was also shown that the social web even creates an additional phase, the so-called need generation: with all of its reviews, personal experiences and holiday photos, the social web may create the need for holidays and hence accommodation in the first place. Also, the after-sale evaluation is especially impacted by the social web where experiences can be shared with the whole online world.

339 Cf. Egger et al. 2010, p. 22f., in: Lassnig et al. 2010

With their presence on the social web, hotels are active within the same surroundings as their guests. As they may get into direct contact, they create awareness for their services. Considering that the information search is narrowed down to certain sites during the filtering process, hotels should try to influence that filter. With regards to the AIDA concept, the hotels' social web presences should create attention and interest resulting in decision and action, with the final booking preferably on the hotel website. With all these measures, hotels should try to become a part of the social graph, which is an individual travel companion and influencer according to Amersdorffer et al.[340]

The Internet has developed into the most important tourist information source and into a significant booking method. Also, the information search is influenced by the social web. Currently, mostly review sites are significant; other social web applications are important information sources to a rather small share of users. Mostly, the social web is used passively.

In order to characterize the environment of the later empirical study, the next chapter will present the German hotel market.

340 Cf. Amersdorffer et al. 2010, p. 8f., in: Amersdorffer et al. 2010

4 The German Hotel Market

4.1 Market Overviews

As this paper is investigating the information process of hotel guests, the framework is embedded in the hotel industry. Therefore, the following explanations present the German hotel market in order to create an understanding for the specific structure of it as well as to integrate the study into the right context.

The tourism industry is the worldwide biggest commercial sector and accounts for 11% of the worldwide GDP.[341] The lodging industry represents a core of the tourism economy[342] as the following figure depicts:

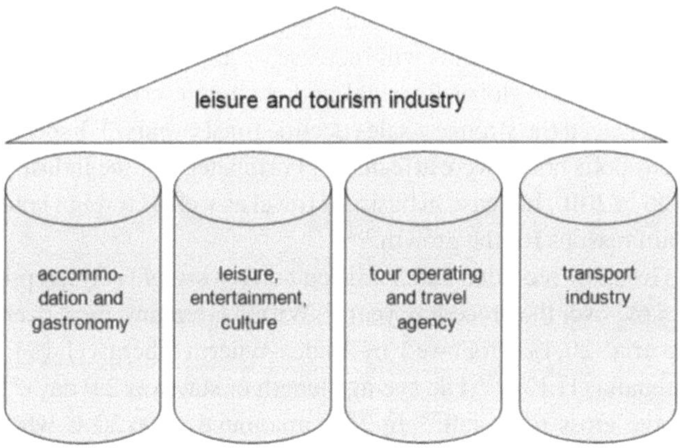

Fig. 20: Four Pillars of the Leisure and Tourism Industry. Source: Quack et al.[343]

The classic lodging industry is made up of hotels, hotels garni, inns and guest houses.[344] The Deutsche Hotel und Gaststättenverband e.V. (DEHOGA) defines the term hotel as follows: 'A hotel is a lodging establishment with a reception, where services, daily room cleaning, additional facilities as well as at least one restaurant for hotel guests and passers-by are offered. A hotel should provide more than 20 guest rooms.'[345]

341 Cf. Eisenstein et al. 2003, p. 805, in: Becker et al. 2003

342 Cf. Quack et al. 2003, p. 359, in: Becker et al. 2003

343 Quack et al. 2003, p. 360, in: Becker et al. 2003

344 Cf. IHA 2011, p. 33

345 DEHOGA 2011 (author's translation)

In December 2010, there were 13,779 hotels, 8,164 hotels garni, 9,035 inns and 5,675 guest houses in Germany.[346] In total, 940,484 guest rooms were offered, of which 578,550 were hotel rooms.[347] The great majority of all guest rooms of the lodging industry is hence made up by hotel rooms. The most classified hotels (as of January 2011) belong to the three-star category (4,845), followed by the four-star category (2,293), the two-star category (731), the five-star category (134) and the one-star category (62).[348] Because hotels do not need a DEHOGA classification in order to operate, these figures only refer to the classified hotels (the total number of classified hotels in 2011: 8,065).[349] The German lodging industry is predominantly characterized by small businesses and only 7% of the German hotels offer more than 100 rooms.[350] Until the end of 2013 another 431 hotel projects (new buildings, building refurbishments and enlargements) are planned; if all of these projects are realized, the offer of hotel rooms will increase by another 64,965 rooms.[351]

In 2009, the year of global financial and economic crisis, the German hotel industry experienced the strongest sales decline for six years.[352] Especially conference and metropolis hotels were affected.[353] Fortunately for the industry, the situation improved in 2010. Increase in business travel as well as foreign hotel bookings were the main reasons for the growth.[354]

In 2010, Germany recorded 228.3 million hotel overnight stays, representing an increase of 5.6% over the preceding year.[355] Within Germany, most overnight stays were in Bavaria (20.4%), followed by Baden-Wuerttemberg (11.4%) and North Rhine-Westphalia (11.1%).[356] The average length of stay was 2.0 days.[357]

The average gross room rate[358] in 2010 amounted to 96.30 € while the average net room rate[359] in 2010 amounted to 90 € and increased by 12.6% compared

346 Cf. IHA 2011, p. 33

347 Cf. IHA 2011, p. 33

348 Cf. IHA 2011, p. 33

349 Cf. IHA 2011, p. 190

350 Cf. IHA 2011, p. 34

351 Cf. IHA 2011, p. 6

352 Cf. DEHOGA 2010, p.2

353 Cf. IHA 2011, p. 13

354 Cf. DEHOGA 2010, p. 2

355 Cf. IHA 2011, p. 49

356 Cf. IHA 2011, p. 49

357 Cf. IHA 2011, p. 55

358 Including value-added tax without breakfast

359 Excluding value-added tax without breakfast

to 2009.[360] The comparatively higher net room rate in 2010 was favoured by the reduction of value-added tax from 19% to 7% since January 2010.[361] The highest net room rates were paid in Munich and Frankfurt (113 €), followed by Dusseldorf (104 €), Hamburg (100 €) and Stuttgart (99 €).[362] In Europe, the highest net room rates were recorded in Paris with 171 €, followed by London with 149 € and Rome with 139 €.[363]

The most important source market for the German hotel industry is Germany. Around 78.8% of all accommodations in 2010 were generated by German guests, while 21.2% were generated by foreign guests.[364] The second most important source market was the Netherlands with 10.5 million room nights, followed by the USA with 4.7 and the United Kingdom and Switzerland with 4.1 million room-nights each.[365]

In 2010, the average room occupancy rate in Germany was 63.4%; the European occupancy rate reached 63.7%.[366] The cities with the highest occupancy rates were London (82.1%), Edinburgh (76.6%) and Paris (76.3%).[367]

The German hotel market is characterized by great overcapacities. Every night in 2010, more than half a million hotel beds remained empty.[368] Hotel products are getting more and more homogeneous and in general do not offer significant possibilities for a USP. Therefore, the USP may be based on the service. The hotel's communication strategy can be defined as one part of the service. It is not limited to the communication during the hotel stay but also comprises the pre- and post-stay communication. The social web can be a crucial factor to improve communication strategy and to create a USP in the long term.

360 Cf. IHA 2011, p. 6
361 Cf. IHA 2011, p. 17
362 Cf. IHA 2011, p. 21
363 Cf. IHA 2011, p. 23
364 Cf. IHA 2011, p. 52
365 Cf. IHA 2011, p. 54
366 Cf. IHA 2011, p. 23
367 Cf. IHA 2011, p. 23
368 Cf. IHA 2011, p. 34

The demand side in the hotel industry is characterized by many trends,[369] of which the following may be influenced by the social web:

- increasing aspiration level of the guests
- increasing education level, travel experience and travel frequency
- critical consciousness of the guests
- increasing experience orientation
- decreasing risk tolerance
- increasing flexibility
- decreasing customer loyalty.

Due to their increasing travel experience guests become more demanding. A hotel accommodation is not only an overnight stay but rather an experience and guests expect certain services far beyond the actual core service. With the help of reviews and experiences by others, guests may evaluate the hotel's services in advance, which is highly decreasing the willingness to carry risks. Through the social web guests easily receive information about the hotel and can get in contact with it. Also, the travel behaviour is changing, becoming more flexible. The social web also offers possibilities for last-minute marketing activities. As generally a decreasing customer loyalty can be witnessed, the social web provides opportunities to engage in unique and sophisticated dialogues with the guests, thereby reincreasing their loyalty.

4.2 Distribution Policy

The following paragraphs will investigate the distribution policy of the hotel market in order to demonstrate that there is a great need for the increase in direct bookings. This increase may also be induced by the social web.

The distribution policy is an essential part of the marketing mix. Since the services can only be used at the hotel site, the '[…] main task of the distribution policy is to sell the entitlement to benefits'.[370] Hotels can avail themselves of different distribution channels which can be classified into direct channels, where the

369 Cf. Gardini 2003, p. 59

370 Hänssler 2008, p. 259 (author's translation)

hotel sells its services directly to the guest, and indirect channels, where at least one sales intermediary is interposed.[371]

The following diagram shows the indirect distribution:

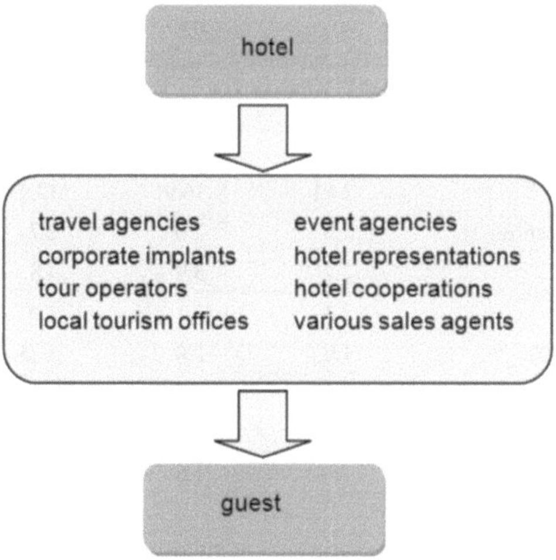

Fig. 21: Process of Indirect Hotel Booking. Source: Hänssler[372]

Although the indirect distribution is more expensive, it is connected with certain advantages: the biggest advantage is that the services can be sold region-wide as the intermediaries have a higher outreach than the hotel alone.[373] Furthermore, existing customers of the intermediary can be approached. Mostly, costs only arise with the booking and are therefore variable and profit-related.[374] Another distinction can be made between online and offline distribution. The offline distribution comprises the bookings via phone and fax, mail, personal bookings, the walk-in guest that arrives without any prior reservation as well as the bookings being made via a travel agency or tour operator; the online distribution comprises the booking on the hotel homepage, the booking via other Internet portals and via email.[375] The following table shows the shares of different distribution channels of German hotels from 2003 to 2009:

371 Cf. Hänssler 2008, p. 259

372 Hänssler 2008, p. 263 (author's translation)

373 Cf. Hänssler 2008, p. 263

374 Cf. Hänssler 2008, p. 263

375 Cf. IHA 2011, p. 156

rank	distribution channel	share 2003 in %	share 2005 in %	share 2007 in %	share 2009 in %
1	Internet portals	4.1	7.1	9.9	**24.7**
2	own homepage	2.0	5.9	6.0	**22.6**
3	email	5.9	9.7	11.3	10.8
4	phone	32.2	29.0	20.5	9.9
5	GDS[a]	8.1	8.6	5.4	8.7
6	tour operator	10.7	8.5	10	6.3
7	telefax	24.1	16.9	13.5	5.8
8	own call centre	2.3	2.0	2.7	4.6
9	walk in	2.7	3.9	4.8	2.6
10	letter	2.1	2.1	2.5	1.5
11	CRS (own)[b]	1.0	2.0	11.3	0.8
12	CRS (foreign)	0.7	1.0	0.8	0.8
13	others	3.1	1.8	0.3	0.8
14	tourist marketing org.	1.0	1.6	0.9	0.6

a. Global distribution system.

b. Central reservation system. The strong decrease of the own CRS bookings since 2007 is explained by the fact that in 2009 own CRS bookings were calculated to the homepage bookings (Cf. IHA 2011, p. 156).

Table 9: Share of Distribution Channels from 2003 to 2009. Source: IHA[376]

The table shows that Internet portals were the most important distribution channel in 2009 with a share of 24.7%. In 2003, this share amounted to only 4.1%, which implies a great increase within the last six years. The second most important distribution channel in 2009 was the hotel homepage with 22.6%. Altogether, the Internet portals, hotel homepages and emails made up more than 50% of all bookings in 2009. However, the costs between these three channels greatly differ as indirect bookings are connected with high provisions. The following table shows the provisions by the different distribution channels:

376 IHA 2011, p. 156

distribution channel	**homepage: free booking engine**	**retail inter-mediary via Extranet**	**intermediary via Pegasus**	**travel agency via GDS**	**online portal via GDS**	**wholesaler direct**	**opaque (hidden price) via GDS**
example	Muster-Hotel.de	hrs.de hotel.de	eHotel.de hotel.de	CWT, Amex	orbitz.de,	expedia.at	priceline.com
booking value	150 €	150 €	150 €	150 €	150 €	150 €	150 €
booking fee	0 €	0 €	0 €	0 €	6 €	4 €	4 €
provision	0%	10%	8%	0%	0%	0%	0%
estimated mark up	0%	0%	0%	0%	0%	25%	25%
travel agency com-mission	0%	0%	0%	10%	10%	0%	0%
CRS & switch	0 €	0 €	0 €	8 €	8 €	0 €	8 €
GDS	0 €	0 €	0 €	5 €	5 €	0 €	5 €
credit card	2.5%	2.5%	2.5%	2.5%	2.5%	0% (Voucher)	0% (Voucher)
reservation costs	3.75 €	18.75 €	15.75 €	31.75 €	37.75 €	41.50 €	54.50 €
lodgings revenue	146.25 €	131.25 €	134.25 €	118.25 €	112.25 €	108.50 €	95.50 €
total costs	**2.5%**	**13%**	**11%**	**21%**	**25%**	**28%**	**36%**

Table 10: Provisions by Distribution Channel. Source: IHA[377]

377 IHA 2011, p. 158

As the table clearly shows, the costs between the different booking possibilities differ greatly. The cheapest possibility by far is the direct booking via the hotel's homepage. The aim of the distribution policy should hence be to generate as many direct bookings as possible. Bookings via third parties have to be seen critically due to two main reasons. The first reason is the already addressed rentability of the bookings. The second reason concerns the guest's loyalty. While making a booking on booking sites the guest is exposed to many hotels. The probability of changing the hotel – even if positive previous experiences exist – is therefore higher.

4.3 Summary

The German hotel market is characterized by a varied landscape from small and individually run hotels to huge hotel resorts and big hotel chains. Predominantly, the market is made up of small businesses and only 7% of the German hotels offer more than 100 rooms.[378] As the social web is available to all hotels, independent from their size and financial resources, it may represent an attractive communication channel, especially for smaller hotels which generally have less budget for marketing activities.

On the German hotel market great overcapacities avail with an average room occupancy rate of 63.4% in 2010.[379] As the competition is extremely fierce, hotels need to have a USP in order to distinguish themselves from their competitors. This USP can also be created with a diversified communication on the social web. Most of today's bookings are already generated through the Internet, therefore the majority of all guests is online when booking a hotel. As the social web generally has become an integrated part of most of the people's daily lives, hotels may easily engage with their customers in their familiar surroundings. Additionally, the demand side is characterized by certain trends, out of which many, e.g. the decreasing customer loyalty, may be positively influenced by a participation in the social web.

As shown in table 10, indirect bookings are connected with high provisions. The bookings with the least costs to the hotels are those made on the hotel's homepage. However, this distribution channel had a booking share of only 22.6% in 2009,[380] thereby showing great future potential. The ultimate aim of the distribution policy should be to increase direct bookings, which may be supported by the social web.

378 Cf. IHA 2011, p. 34

379 Cf. IHA 2011, p. 23

380 Cf. IHA 2011, p. 156

With the discussion of the current Internet and social web usage, followed by the presentation of selected information models and the German hotel market, the theoretical foundation for the paper has been laid. In the following the methodology and empirical study will be presented.

5 Methodology

5.1 Presentation of the Example Case

The empirical research was conducted in cooperation with a hotel chain in Germany. The portfolio of the hotel chain includes business hotels in Germany's biggest cities as well as spa resorts in popular holiday destinations. The hotels mostly belong to the three- and four-star category. The surveyed guests – both leisure and business guests – meet the following requirements:

- at least one hotel stay at a German hotel
- German-speaking and residence in Germany
- email address available.

The survey group received the questionnaire as a part of a monthly email newsletter, in which three offers as well as the survey were promoted. In order to attract as many guests as possible, participation was connected with a raffle in which two overnight stays with breakfast and other services could be won.

5.2 Research Approach and Study Design

In order to test the previously presented research hypotheses, primary research has been conducted. For the successful conduction of the field research, the following chapter will clarify important principles.

5.2.1 Research Method

Guest surveys are an essential component of tourist market research. By means of guest surveys, information for demand and offer, competition and image analysis may be gathered.[381] For this paper, a demand analysis is conducted.

381 Cf. Bosold 1993, p. 539f., in: Hahn et al. 1993

The following four research methods can be applied when conducting analyses in the lodging industry:[382]

- survey
- exploration
- observation
- experiment.

The information process is predominantly an internal process which cannot be well analyzed by observation and exploration, as artificial framework conditions need to be created: the subject group would have to be 'forced' to search for information on the social web at the time of empiricism, which could distort the results. For this paper, the survey has been chosen as the applied research method, as it is highly applicable to the field of investigation.

The questioning technique of a survey is divided into written and oral investigations. The written survey can further be categorized in postal, directly completed on site and online submissions; the oral survey consists of in-person questioning and telephone inquiries.[383] Independent from the type, all surveys are usually based on a questionnaire. A questionnaire can be described as a '[…] more or less standardized composition of questions that are posed to people. Analysis of the answers should prove or disprove theoretical concepts and correlations. The questionnaire is hence the central link between theory and analysis.'[384]

Compared to the oral inquiry, written surveys offer different advantages. The biggest advantage is the small manpower requirement, as the interviewer does not have to be present during the time of investigation.[385] So-called interviewer effects, e.g. biases, are omitted.[386] The interviewees are not put under any time pressure and can answer the questions at their convenience. Therefore, the time frame also has to be larger because the time for returning the questionnaires has to be considered.[387] During the survey, participants may decide to discontinue the survey. However, after the three to four first questions have been answered, the

382 Cf. Gardini 2003, p. 77f.

383 Cf. Jacob et al. 2011, p. 104

384 Porst 2011, p. 14 (author's translation)

385 Cf. Jacob et al. 2011, p. 112

386 Cf. Jacob et al. 2011, p. 113

387 Cf. Jacob et al. 2011, p. 112

probability of discontinuation is rather low.[388] Therefore, the opening questions are of special importance.

A special type of written survey is the online survey, whose importance has drastically increased within the last decade.[389] Online surveys are inquiries that are conducted '[…] with the use of the Internet'.[390] Generally, there are three types of online surveys:[391]

- anonymous surveys (subject group is not pre-determined)
- personalized surveys (subject group is pre-determined and email addresses exist)
- panel-based surveys (only members in a certain panel are being questioned).

The most commonly used type of online inquiries are personalized surveys.[392] One great advantage of the online questionnaire is the rather low financial effort because printing and mailing costs are being omitted. Furthermore, the data entry can be often done automatically, which drastically decreases the manpower requirement for the later evaluation.[393] The actual costs when conducting an online survey are limited to the contentual and conceptual creation of the survey as well as the costs for the server and survey software.[394] Therefore, an online survey can be done up to 70% cheaper than postal inquiries.[395] Additionally, online surveys can be conducted much faster because the questionnaires do not have to be sent back. Jacob et al.[396] recommends a time frame of two to three weeks for online surveys. In addition, multimedia effects as well as automatic filtering can be included.[397] The biggest disadvantage of online surveys is that only the online population can be questioned.[398] Hence, not every topic is suitable for online surveys. However, this disadvantage does not apply to Internet-specific topics. Summing

388 Cf. Porst 2011, p. 135
389 Cf. Jacob et al. 2011, p. 116
390 Gräf 2010, p. 9 (author's translation)
391 Cf. Gräf 2010, p. 15
392 Cf. Gräf 2010, p. 21
393 Cf. Jacob et al. 2011, p. 116
394 Cf. Jacob et al. 2011, p. 116
395 Cf. Jacob et al. 2011, p. 116
396 Cf. Jacob et al. 2011, p. 116
397 Cf. Jacob et al. 2011, p. 117
398 Cf. Jacob et al. 2011, p. 121

up, the online survey offers important technical, financial and methodological advantages.
In addition to general methodological requirements for questionnaires, further aspects have to be considered when conducting an online survey. One great difference between postal and online questionnaires is the display. It is recommended to begin with a welcome page, in order to evoke a feeling of a dialogue.[399] The front page should present the participating company, institute or person and give a brief introduction into the topic area; furthermore, anonymity and data privacy should be mentioned.[400]

Having weighed all of the possibilities, the online questionnaire is finally chosen for this paper due to its various advantages. Furthermore, the topic of the survey is the social web, which requires an online presence. The often applied criticism regarding questionnaires about the information behaviour – the survey is conducted after the actual information search and can only consider the conscious and controlled parts thereof[401] – is accepted.

5.2.2 *Interrogative Form*

After having chosen the research method, the structure of the questionnaire has to be determined. Questions can be differentiated by their content and their form.[402] One can divide questions into categorical and ordinal types.[403] Categorical questions can be applied for questions with a nominal scale. Common types are alternative questions or questions with only two answers. Ordinal questions scrutinize the expression of characteristics in order to bring them into a certain ranking, e.g. the degree of satisfaction.[404]

The structure can be either closed or open. Closed questions predetermine the answer possibilities while open questions leave space for individual answers. Hybrid questions combine open and closed questions. In addition to predetermined answers, interviewees can also give an individual answer. Whereas open questions can often better measure the perception of the participants,[405] closed questions can be evaluated more easily and can be answered independently from the test per-

399 Cf. Gräf 2010, p. 80
400 Cf. Porst 2011, p. 34
401 Cf. Egger et al. 2010, p. 27, in: Lassnig et al. 2010
402 Cf. Porst 2011, p. 51
403 Cf. Jacob et al. 2011, p. 163f.
404 Cf. Jacob et al. 2011, p. 163f.
405 Cf. Jacob et al. 2011, p. 103

son's articulation possibilities.[406] In addition, the answers can be better compared with each other. Furthermore, closed questions have the advantage that they can be answered exclusively with the computer mouse.[407] The HTML standards differentiate between radio buttons, that should be used when asking single choice questions, and check boxes that should be applied when asking multiple-choice questions:[408]

radio buttons: ❍ check boxes: ❑

Closed questions are answered with scales. A scale is a reference frame on which the measuring procedure is based.[409] Scales can be divided into nominal, ordinal, interval and ratio scales. The answer possibilities of nominal scales exclude each other,[410] e.g., 'Was your last hotel stay in a Best Western, Marriott or NH Hotel?'. Means cannot be calculated, neither can a rank be created.[411] Ordinal scales predetermine answers that correlate with each other and underlie a certain rank.[412] However, the distances between the answers are not the same. Interval scales on the other hand have the same distances and a typical interval scale is the Celsius temperature scale.[413] Ratio scales are similar to interval scales but have a zero point.[414] Scales can be verbalized, meaning that every point of scale is explained with a description.[415] The advantage is that the scale's points are clearly defined and cannot be interpreted individually; the disadvantage is that the differences between each points are not the same.[416] One could also define the endpoints of a scale only, however, then the participants could interpret the points in between differently.[417] The scale can be odd or even. Odd scales involve the risk that participants may also see the centre of the scale as the contentual centre and choose

406 Cf. Gräf 2010, p. 76
407 Cf. Gräf 2010, p. 48
408 Cf. Gräf 2010, p. 48
409 Cf. Porst 2011, p. 69
410 Cf. Porst 2011, p. 69
411 Cf. Jacob et al. 2011, p. 35
412 Cf. Porst 2011, p. 71
413 Cf. Porst 2011, p. 72
414 Cf. Porst 2011, p. 74
415 Cf. Porst 2011, p. 78
416 Cf. Porst 2011, p. 78
417 Cf. Porst 2011, p. 80

it when being uncertain; on even scales, survey participants cannot choose the central position, even if they would tend to do so.[418]

Matrix questions are tabular questions; they are structured in a way that every row is connected with a certain question and every column is connected with predetermined answer possibilities.[419] Matrix questions can summarize different questions in one question set. In general, they can be answered faster and need less space. Matrix questions should be displayed on one screen page without the necessity to scroll.[420]

In addition to these mentioned requirements, the participant has to understand the questions in terms of wording and in terms of content.[421] Also, the dramaturgy should be considered and questions dealing with the same topic should be asked in one passage.[422]

5.2.3 *Creation of the Questionnaire*

The questionnaire has been created with regard to the formerly mentioned requirements. The survey's landing page includes a greeting with the presentation of the topic and the participating institutions.

The questions used are categorical and ordinal questions. Only closed questions are posed. The answers are displayed on nominal and ordinal scales. The use of the different social web channels is surveyed with matrix questions. Every theme section is presented on a new page. Interviewees can answer all questions without scrolling down or up.

Automatic filtering is included at the beginning where participants that state that they do not use the social web at all are forwarded to the demographic part at the end. A progressing display is used to inform the interviewees about the remaining parts. Participants are not forced to answer every question but can skip questions at their convenience.

The structure of the topics dealt with in the questionnaire is as follows:[423]

418 Cf. Porst 2011, p. 81

419 Cf. Gräf 2011, p. 42

420 Cf. Gräf 2011, p. 44

421 Cf. Porst 2011, p. 21f.

422 Cf. Porst 2011, p. 142

423 The complete questionnaire can be found in the appendix.

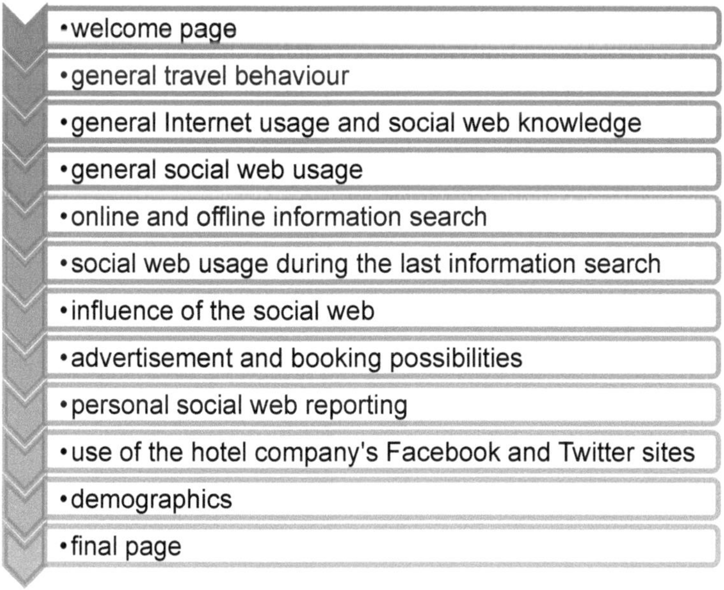

Fig. 22: Structure of the Questionnaire. Source: own survey

The (informational) use of the following social web applications is questioned:[424]

- hotel review sites
- social networks
- travel communities
- media sharing platforms
- blogs & podcasts
- microblogs
- travel communities
- booking sites with review function.[425]

424 The questionnaire is orientated on Raab 2012.

425 Examples for booking sites with review function are hrs.de and booking.com. Although these sites predominantly present a booking site, they include also the possibility of reviewing the hotel stay and were therefore included in the questionnaire.

In order to eliminate all contentual and technical mistakes, a pretest was undertaken with students at the University of Trier during the seminar 'Kommunikation im Tourismus' taught in the winter semester 2011/2012.

6 Results of the Survey

6.1 Emailing and Participation in the Questionnaires

The questionnaire was sent out on Friday, 20th January 2012 as a part of a monthly hotel newsletter. The link leading to the questionnaire registered 1,293 unique clicks. In total, 940 participants completed the questionnaire. Since the participants could skip questions at their convenience, not every question received a response rate of 100%. The possibility of a double participation was not technically inhibited, however is considered to be small.

The highest drop-out rate was registered on the welcome page. This can be explained by the fact that the newsletter mentioned only the questionnaire but not its topic, therefore the potential participants did not know its theme. While 1,293 recipients of the newsletter clicked on the survey, 940 finished the questionnaire completely. Assuming that every user only participated in the questionnaire once, this represents a response rate of 72.7%. This number shows that there is a great interest in this topic.

The highest participation rate was generated on the day of dispatch with 51.1%, followed by the 21st January with 19.03% and the 23rd with 14.93%. Hence 85.06% of all finished questionnaires were generated in the first four days. In order to receive the highest participation rate possible, the questionnaire was available for two weeks before the analyses began.

6.2 Frequency Distribution

6.2.1 General Information about the Sample Group

From the total of 940 participants, 51.5% are male while 48.5% are female. Hence, the target group is almost made up equally by men and women. The best represented age groups are 41 to 45 years and 36 to 40 years. In total, 72% of the participants are aged between 31 and 55 years. However, also participants aged 60 years and older are well represented with over 15%. Differentiated between genders and age groups, the age groups 51 to 75 years are slightly more represented by male participants. For all other age groups no distinct differences can be observed.[426]

The great majority is working (74.8%), followed by retirees and pupils, students and trainees. The following table gives an overview of the demographic composition of the sample group:

---

426 Complete differentiation between genders and age groups can be found in the appendix.

characteristic	distinctness	number	in %
gender	male	467	51.5%
	female	440	48.5%
	total	940	100%
age	18 to 25	18	2.0%
	26 to 30	29	3.2%
	31 to 35	119	13.0%
	36 to 40	142	15.5%
	41 to 45	159	17.3%
	46 to 50	123	13.4%
	51 to 55	117	12.8%
	56 to 60	67	7.3%
	61 to 65	39	4.3%
	66 to 70	10	1.1%
	71 to 75	39	4.3%
	76 and older	55	6.0%
	total	917	100.2%
occupation	pupil/student/trainee	13	1.4%
	employed	684	74.8%
	unemployed	49	5.4%
	retiree	169	18.5%
	total	915	100.1%

Table 11: Demographic Composition of the Sample Group. Source: own survey

The majority (71.1%) of hotel overnight stays occurs due to private reasons while 28.9% of the accommodations are business-related. The participants have a high travel frequency and 45.6% have five and more hotel stays per year, while 38.3% have three to four stays. The differentiation between travel purpose and travel frequency reveals that frequent travellers are almost equally made up by leisure and business guests while guests with one to four hotel stays per year are mostly leisure guests:

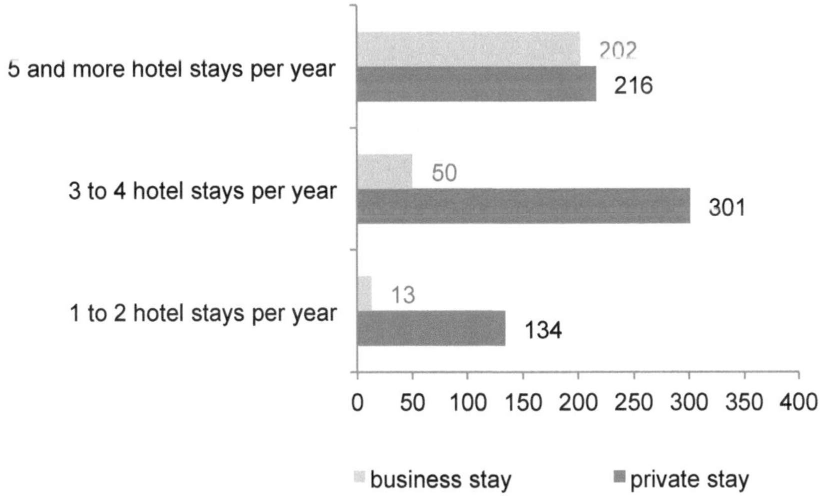

Fig. 23: Travel Frequency by Travel Occasion. Source: own survey

The most frequently used booking methods are the hotel homepage,[427] third-party online providers and the reservation by telephone directly at the hotel. The following diagram presents the used booking methods of the participants graphically:

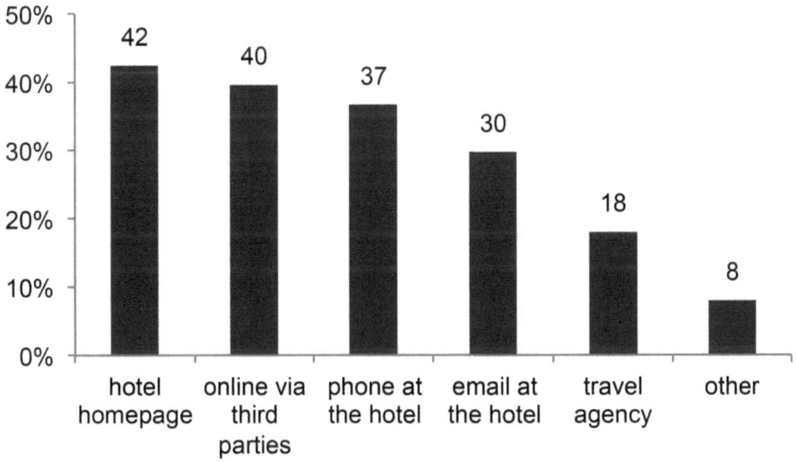

Fig. 24: Booking Methods. Multiple responses possible. Source: own survey

427 The high acceptance of the hotel homepage as a booking channel is judged very positively, as this booking method is connected with the fewest costs (view chapter 4.2).

12.7% of the participants book via a smartphone or tablet pc.

In summary, the ratio of men and women in the sample group is rather equal and all age groups are represented with the majority of participants aged between 31 and 55 years. As the majority has a high travel frequency, the participants are considered suitable for investigating hotel information processes. The following subchapter will highlight the Internet usage and travel information behaviour of the participants.

6.2.2 Internet Usage and Information Behaviour

The sample group shows a very high Internet affinity: 87.9% use the Internet daily, 10.1% several times a week and 1.5% weekly, hence 99.5% access the Internet at least weekly. The classification by age groups reveals that there are no significant differences regarding the Internet frequency of use by age groups. Neither can a distinct difference in Internet use be found between genders. The Internet is mainly used privately and accessed with a computer or laptop from home (63.3%). The high Internet affinity results in a profound knowledge: 72.6% of the participants are familiar with the term social web. However, there are strong differences in social web usage as the following figure depicts:

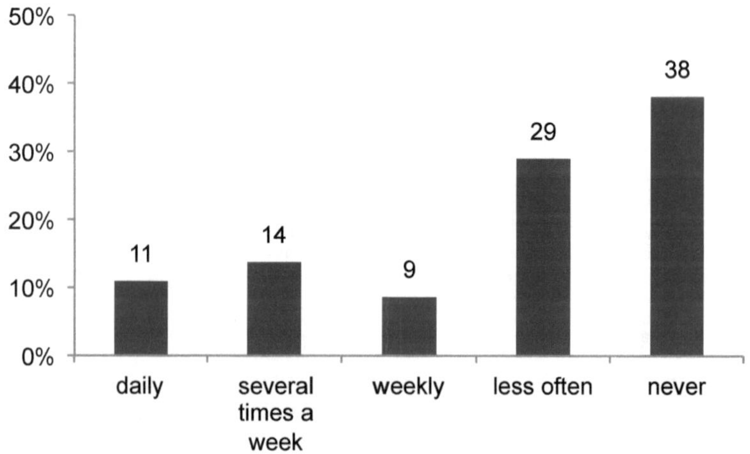

Fig. 25: Frequency of Using the Social Web. Source: own survey

Although the relative majority (38%) never uses the social web,[428] at least 34% access it daily, several times a week or weekly. With regard to travel occasion and gender, no distinct differences can be found. However, there are great differences between age groups:[429]

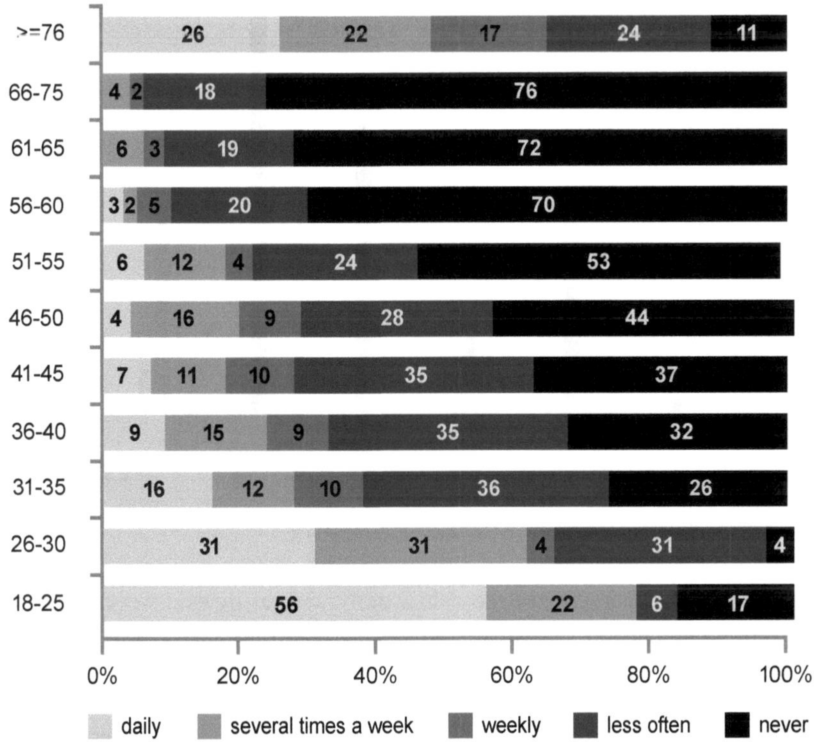

Fig. 26: General Social Web Usage by Age. Source: own survey

The figure clearly shows that the frequency of using the social web decreases with increasing age.[430] While there are almost 80% of users aged between 18 and 25

428 Users who state that they do not use the social web at all are excluded from all analyses regarding the information process and informational social web usage, as they were automatically forwarded to the demographic part.

429 Age groups 66 to 70 and 71 to 75 are united due to the small number of participants in the age group 66 to 70 years.

430 Participants aged 76 and older show a very intense social web usage, especially compared to the age group 66 to 75. Because age was one of the last questions in the survey and answer *76 and*

years that access the social web at least several times a week, there are only 6% aged between 66 and 75 years who use it to the same extent. The following figure depicts the use of the different social web sites:[431]

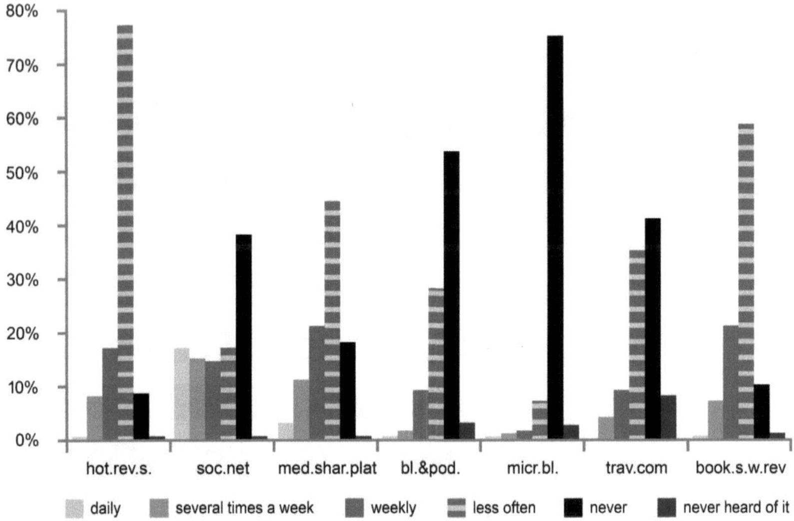

Fig. 27: Social Web Sites Frequency of Use. Source: own survey

The applications accessed the most on a daily, several times a week or weekly basis are social networks (45%). Media sharing platforms and booking sites with review function follow with 36% resp. 30%. Hotel review sites are accessed by 25% on a weekly basis while travel communities and blogs & podcasts are used by 14% and 13%. Microblogs follow as the last with 5% (multiple responses possible). Although these numbers certainly show an active participation in the social web, it has to be acknowledged that there are many participants who do not use the surveyed social web sites at all.

The Internet plays an important role for the hotel information process: 59% of all participants state that they are looking for information online, as the following figure presents:

older was the last box to tick, it may be theoretically possible that users chose that box only out of convenience. In order to prevent incorrect conclusions regarding best agers in general, the age group 76 and older is excluded from all following calculations where the age is considered.

431 For reasons of clarity the different values are not presented.

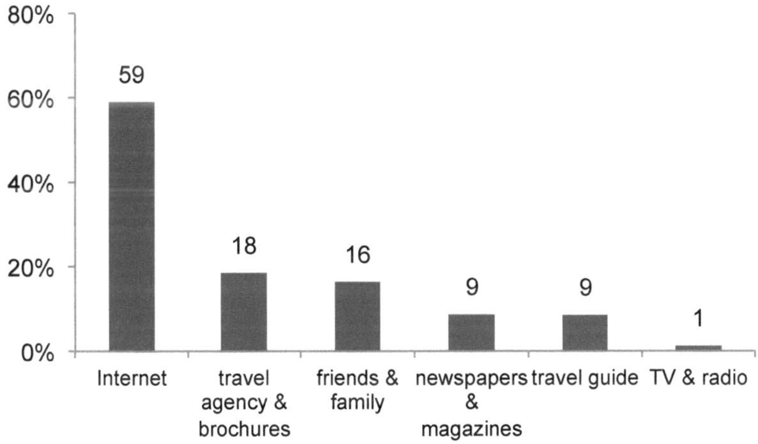

Fig. 28: General Information Sources. Multiple responses possible. Source: own survey

The Internet is by far the most important information source. Travel agency & brochures and friends & family follow with a great distance. Newspapers & magazines as well as travel guides are used only by a rather small share for hotel information gathering. Television and radio do not play a role at all.

When searching online, the majority of the participants accesses hotel homepages (88%). Booking sites with review function[432] are the second (56%) and the social web[433] the third (23%) most important online information sources, followed by destination sites (19%). Apps are mostly not considered at all (3%) (multiple responses possible).

When questioned about the social web applications used during the hotel information gathering, the participants mentioned the following usage:

432 Although booking sites with review function were defined as belonging to the social web, they were surveyed separately for this question, as the social aspects – the reviewing function – of these sites do not necessarily have to be used.

433 For this question only 23% of the considered users stated to use the social web as a source of information. However, when questioning the informational use of specific social web sites, the percentual usage increases (view figure 29).

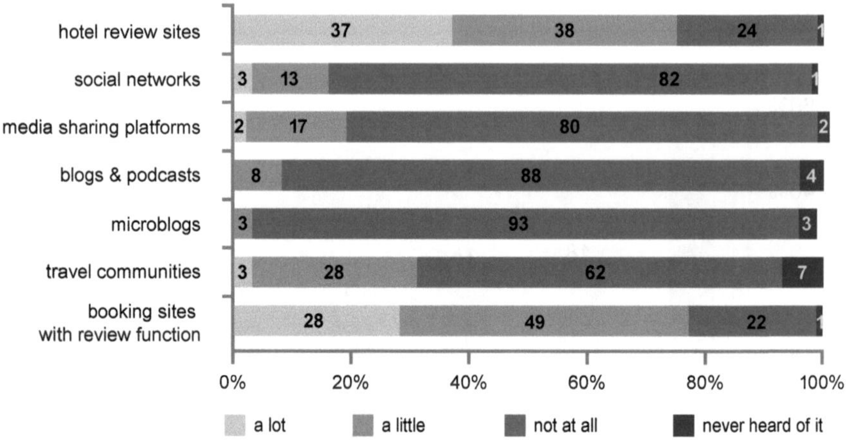

Fig. 29: Social Web Sites Used for Hotel Information Search. Source: own survey

The most important information sites are booking sites with review function and hotel review sites which 77% resp. 75% at least used a little. Travel communities are used by 31%, media sharing platforms by 19% and social networks by 16%. The figure clearly shows that microblogs and blogs & podcasts are not used as an information source by the great majority of the participants.

Reviews on the social web have a significant impact on the personal booking decision and 27.1% have already withdrawn their existing booking decision due to negative reviews. However, the impact differs greatly between the different social web applications:

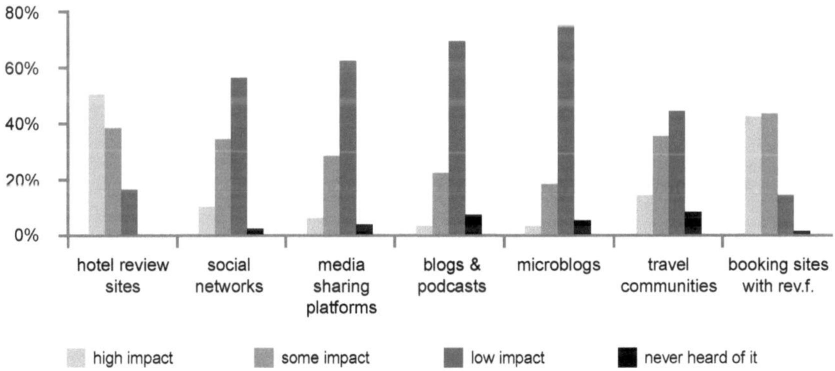

Fig. 30: Impact of Social Web Sites on the Personal Booking Decision[434]*. Source: own survey*

According to the chart, participants acknowledged that hotel review sites (87.4%) and booking sites with review function (84.1%) have a high impact to some impact on the booking decision. Next are travel communities which have high/some impact on 50.1% of the participants. Social networks are also crucial and 10.5% state high and 31.6% some impact. The same can be said of media sharing platforms with 6.5% claiming high impact and 27.9% reporting some. Very few of those surveyed listed blogs & podcasts (2%) and microblogs (2.9%) as having high impact on the booking decision. The some impact percentage for these sources were 22.9% and 19.1% resp. However, there is also a great number of participants whose booking decision is only very little influenced by social web reviews.

The majority of the sample group uses the social web during the information process passively. However, there are also active contributors (at least occasional reporting): 44.6% publish reviews on hotel review sites, 42.6% on booking sites, 16.9% share experiences on travel communities and 14.9% on social networks. Media sharing platforms, blogs & podcasts and microblogs play an insignificant role for experience sharing on the social web.

434 For reasons of clarity the different values are not presented.

Regarding the objects of information, the following distribution arises:

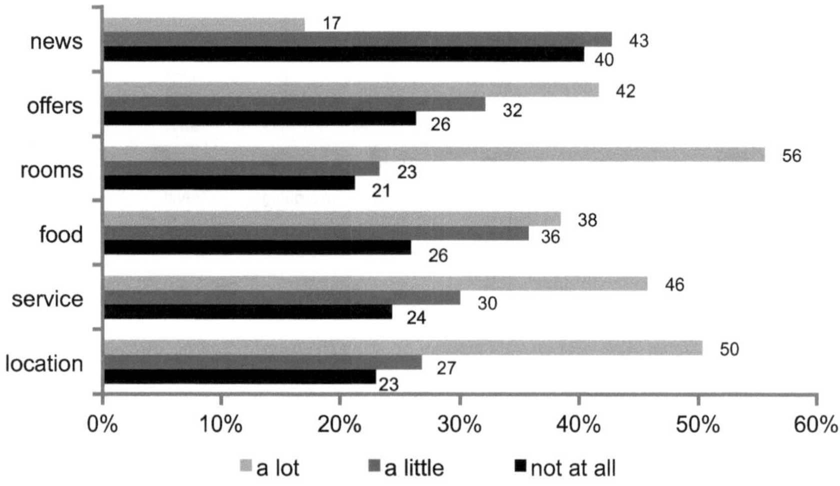

Fig. 31: Objects of Information. Source: own survey

The most sought-after information concerns the location and the rooms, followed by service, food and offers. News about the hotel is the least interesting object of information. Only 4.8% of the participants follow the hotel group on Facebook and 1.2% on Twitter. These numbers show the guests' lack of interest in becoming a fan or follower.

Summing up, the sample group displays a very high Internet affinity with almost every participant accessing it at least weekly. One third also uses the social web at least once a week. Hotel review sites and booking sites with review function are predominantly accessed when using the social web to search for information. Social networks, travel communities and media sharing platforms are also used. The majority of the sample group consists of passive spectators, but there are also active contributors who publish reviews on the social web.

As the questionnaire has been evaluated according to frequency distribution, the following chapter will analyze the results statistically in order to answer the previously presented research hypotheses.

6.3 Statistical Analyses

The following subchapters will statistically test the previously defined research hypotheses. In order to do so, the statistic program SPSS[435] is used. The analyses take place separately for the different research hypotheses

6.3.1 Research Hypothesis I

6.3.1.1 Statistical Analysis of Research Hypothesis I

RH I: The informational social web usage depends on travel frequency and the general social web usage.

The aim of RH I is to find out to what extent differences between frequent and occasional travellers and frequent and occasional social web users regarding their use of the social web as an information source exist.

Regarding travel frequency, it is easy to assume that frequent travellers apply a more advanced hotel information search than occasional travellers, as they have to search for information more often, thereby possibly being more sophisticated concerning the choice of information sources. Additionally, RH I investigates if frequent and occasional social web users access it as a source of information to the same extent. As frequent users are more familiar with the social web's different sites and functions, it is only to be expected that they consider the social web as an information source more than occasional users.

In the following, statistical calculations are conducted. The analyses are carried out first by travel frequency and then by the general social web usage. All analyses are conducted separately for the different social web sites.

Travel Frequency

The first part of RH I analyzes the travel frequency, investigating if the informational use of the social web depends on the number of hotel stays per year.

First, a chi-square test[436] has been conducted, in order to see if there is a relationship between travel frequency and the use of social web sites as a source of information. There is a significant relationship between travel frequency and the degree of using booking sites with review function during the information process

435 Version 19 and 20.

436 The chi-square test after Pearson has been applied for this and all further chi-square calculations.

($p < 0.05$), hence it may be assumed that both variables are related. For all other sites no significant relationship can be defined ($p > 0.05$).

Next, average calculating operations are undertaken:[437] the means[438] for the informational use of the different social web sites are calculated, differentiated by travel frequency:

hotel over-night stays per year		**hot.rev.s.**	**soc.net.**	**med.shar.plat.**	**bl. & pod.**	**micr.bl.**	**tr.comm.**	**book.s.w.rev.**
1-2	mean	**2.05**	2.81	2.82	2.98	2.99	2.76	**2.17**
	N	88	84	84	84	84	84	86
	st. dev.	0.77	0.48	0.44	0.35	0.25	0.57	0.74
3-4	mean	**1.91**	2.84	2.77	2.97	2.99	2.67	**2.03**
	N	215	211	210	204	207	211	212
	st. dev.	0.81	0.49	0.55	0.33	0.29	0.66	0.74
>= 5	mean	**1.82**	2.81	2.83	2.95	2.99	2.74	**1.83**
	N	277	274	273	271	272	270	276
	st. dev.	0.79	0.48	0.44	0.37	0.29	0.62	0.70
total	mean	1.89	2.82	2.81	2.96	2.99	2.72	1.95
	N	580	569	567	559	563	565	574
	st. dev.	0.80	0.49	0.48	0.35	0.28	0.63	0.73

Table 12: Means: Informational Social Web Usage by Travel Frequency. Source: own survey

According to the table, the means of two social web sites differ between frequent and occasional travellers. The means of hotel review sites and booking sites with review function are lower for frequent travellers (mean = 1.82 resp. 1.83) than for

437 Users who state that they do not know some of the surveyed social web sites are purposefully included in all statistical calculations. The analyses were also conducted excluding these users, however, no distinct differences arose. Hence, it was decided to include these users for all following calculations.

438 The means may range from 1 to 4 (1 = used a lot, 2 = used a little, 3 = not used at all, 4 = never heard of it).

occasional travellers (mean = 2.05 resp. 2.17), thereby showing a higher informational use of these sites for frequent travellers. Since guests may not only gather information on these sites but also actually book their hotel rooms, it seems to be consequential that the sites are accessed more often by frequent hotel guests who have to conduct bookings more often. However, the participants were supposed to state the usage for their *last hotel stay* and not for all hotel stays within a certain period, which is why an increasing travel frequency does not necessarily imply a higher usage of these sites. Therefore, differences in means for hotel review and booking sites are noteworthy. For all other social web sites, no great differences in means exist. The means of social networks, travel communities and media sharing platforms are rather high for all travel frequencies, thereby indicating that these sites are used rather scarcely as a source of information. This especially accounts for blogs & podcasts and microblogs, where the means almost reach the value of 3. A t-test[439] conducted for the verification of possible differences between the groups confirms a significant difference for hotel review sites and booking sites with review function ($p < 0.05$).

In order to gain a deeper insight into significant differences between the groups, an analysis of variance (ANOVA)[440] has been carried out.[441] According to the results, the travel frequency has an effect on the informational use of booking sites with review function at the highly significant level of $p = 0.000$.

The ANOVA was followed by an Analysis of Covariance (ANCOVA). The covariate travel frequency has a significant relationship with the informational use of booking sites with review function ($p = 0.000$) and hotel review sites ($p < 0.05$):

439 For the independent t-test occasional travellers are defined with 1 to 2 hotel stays per year while frequent travellers are defined with 3 and more hotel stays per year.

440 It is assumed that the data are scale-levelled. This applies also to all further calculations.

441 This ANOVA and all following ANOVAs are applied, even if the preconditions for running an ANOVA, namely normal distribution and homogeneity of variances, are not always given.

source		**type III sum of square**	**df**	**mean square**	**F**	**sig.**
corrected model	hot.rev.s.	3.164[a]	1	3.164	4.956	**0.026**
	soc.net.	0.029[b]	1	0.029	0.129	0.720
	med.shar.plat.	0.115[c]	1	0.115	0.494	0.482
	bl. & pod.	0.048[d]	1	0.048	0.380	0.538
	micr.bl.	0.006[e]	1	0.006	0.079	0.778
	trav.comm.	0.038[f]	1	0.038	0.096	0.757
	book.s.w.rev.	9.193[g]	1	9.193	17.686	**0.000**
a. R Squared = 0.009 (adjusted R Squared = 0.007)						
b. R Squared = 0.000 (adjusted R Squared = -0.002)						
c. R Squared = 0.001 (adjusted R Squared = -0.001)						
d. R Squared = 0.001 (adjusted R Squared = -0.001)						
e. R Squared = 0.000 (adjusted R Squared = -0.002)						
f. R Squared = 0.000 (adjusted R Squared = -0.002)						
g. R Squared = 0.031 (adjusted R Squared = 0.030)						

Table 13: Test of Between-Subjects Effects: Informational Social Web Usage by Travel Frequency. Source: own survey

Booking sites with review function and hotel review sites are below the significant level of $p < 0.05$ and hence confirm the general significance of the model. However, the values of R Squared for these sites are tending towards zero and hence the variables are not suitable to predict differences.

In order to prove if there is a correlation between the informational social web usage and the travel frequency, a correlation analysis after Pearson[442] has been applied:[443]

442 Since the Pearson correlation coefficient should only be used with interval-scaled data, the variables were also calculated with the Spearman correlation coefficient. Since no significant differences could be detected, the data are deemed to have interval-scaled characteristics. This applies equally to all further correlation calculations.

443 Since both of the variables considered have to run into the same direction from positive to negative resp. high to low, the variable travel frequency was recoded.

		travel frequency	hot.rev.s.	soc.net.	med.shar.plat.	bl. & pod.	micr.bl.	tr.comm.	book.s.w.rev.
travel frequency	correlation after Pearson	1.000	**0.096***[*]	0.010	-0.029	0.026	-0.003	-0.009	**0.177**[**]
	significance (both sides)		0.021	0.816	0.495	0.546	0.944	0.828	0.000
	N	924	580	569	567	559	563	565	574

*The correlation is significant at a level of 0.05 (both sides)

**The correlation is significant at a level of 0.01 (both sides)

Table 14: Pearson Correlation between Travel Frequency and Informational Social Web Usage. Source: own survey

The table presents two significant correlations: there is a positive correlation between travel frequency and the informational use of booking sites with review function with a correlation coefficient of $r = 0.177$ ($p < 0.000$) and between the informational use of hotel review sites with a coefficient of $r = 0.096$ ($p < 0.05$). Both correlation coefficients indicate that the informational use of booking and hotel review sites slightly increases with growing travel frequency. The correlation coefficient of the other social web sites tend towards zero and therefore no correlation can be assumed.

Summing up, the first part of RH I – there exists a relationship between travel frequency and informational use of social web sites – can only be verified with severe limitations. The only two social web channels where a difference in informational usage can be confirmed are hotel review sites and booking sites with review function.

Frequency of Using the Social Web

The second part of RH I considers the general frequency of social web use. The objective is to find out to what extent the informational use of the social web depends on its general frequency of use.

According to the chi-square test, there is a relation between the general frequency of social web use and the informational usage of hotel review sites, social networks, media sharing platforms, travel communities and booking sites with review function ($p < 0.05$). The following table presents the means[444] of the general and informational social web usage:

444 The means may range from 1 to 4 (1 = used a lot, 2 = used a little, 3 = not used at all, 4 = never heard of it).

social web usage		hot.rev.s.	soc.net.	med.shar.plat.	bl. & pod.	micr.bl.	tr.comm.	book.s.w.rev.
daily	mean	**1.78**	**2.52**	**2.76**	3.00	3.00	**2.64**	**1.89**
	N	96	96	96	94	94	95	95
	st. dev.	0.81	0.73	0.61	0.39	0.29	0.71	0.84
several times a week	mean	1.70	2.71	2.76	2.96	2.97	2.61	1.85
	N	123	120	119	118	118	120	123
	st. dev.	0.78	0.54	0.45	0.33	0.29	0.64	0.64
weekly	mean	1.82	2.89	2.74	2.93	3.00	2.54	1.80
	N	77	76	76	72	74	76	76
	st. dev.	0.74	0.35	0.50	0.39	0.23	0.62	0.63
less often	mean	**2.00**	**2.95**	**2.86**	2.96	2.99	**2.84**	**2.05**
	N	262	257	256	255	257	254	258
	st. dev.	0.79	0.30	0.44	0.35	0.30	0.59	0.73
total	mean	1.87	2.82	2.80	2.96	2.99	2.71	1.94
	N	558	549	547	539	543	545	552
	st. dev.	0.79	0.49	0.49	0.36	0.29	0.64	0.72

Table 15: Means: Informational Social Web Usage by General Social Web Usage. Source: own survey

With the exception of blogs & podcasts and microblogs the means increase with decreasing general social web usage, thereby indicating that frequent social web users integrate the social web sites more into their information process than occasional users. This effect is especially strong for social networks, where daily users have a mean of 2.52 while people using the social web less frequently than once a week achieve the mean of 2.95. The t-test[445] confirms the significance of the differences for all sites ($p < 0.05$), except for blogs & podcasts and microblogs ($p > 0.05$). The ANOVA also states a significant effect of the general social web usage on the degree of using hotel review sites, social networks, media sharing platforms, travel communities and booking sites with review function as a source of information ($p < 0.05$).

Next, an ANCOVA has been conducted. The covariate general social web usage has a significant relationship with the informational use of social networks, hotel review sites, travel communities and booking sites with review function ($p < 0.05$):

source		**type III sum of square**	**df**	**mean square**	**F**	**sig.**
corrected model	hot.rev.s.	7.128[a]	1	7.128	11.511	**0.001**
	soc.net.	13.126[b]	1	13.126	62.952	**0.000**
	med.shar.plat.	0.766[c]	1	0.766	3.255	0.072
	bl. & pod.	0.083[d]	1	0.083	0.644	0.423
	micr.bl.	0.000[e]	1	0.000	0.002	0.965
	trav.comm.	4.324[f]	1	4.324	10.850	**0.001**
	book.s.w.rev.	2.120[g]	1	2.120	4.064	**0.044**
a. R Squared = 0.021 (adjusted R Squared = 0.020)						
b. R Squared = **0.107** (adjusted R Squared = 0.105)						
c. R Squared = 0.006 (adjusted R Squared = 0.004)						
d. R Squared = 0.001 (adjusted R Squared = -0.001)						
e. R Squared = 0.000 (adjusted R Squared = -0.002)						
f. R Squared = 0.020 (adjusted R Squared = 0.018)						
g. R Squared = 0.008 (adjusted R Squared = 0.006)						

Table 16: Test of Between-Subjects Effects: Informational Social Web Usage by General Social Web Usage. Source: own survey

445 For the independent t-test frequent social web users are defined as using the social web at least weekly, while occasional users are defined as using it less frequently than once a week.

Except for media sharing platforms, blogs & podcasts and microblogs all sites considered are below the significant level of $p < 0.05$ and hence confirm the significance of the model. Social networks reach the highest R Squared and thereby show that they may be suitable to predict a small amount of differences. As the R Squared for all other sites are tending towards zero, they may not be suitable for predictions.

The correlation analysis confirms the correlation between general social web usage and informational use of all social web sites except for blogs & podcasts and microblogs:

		frequency of using the social web	hot. rev.s.	soc.net.	med.shar.plat.	bl. & pod.	micr.bl.	tr.comm.	book.s.w.rev.
frequency of using the social web	correlation after Pearson	1.000	**0.140******	**0.332******	**0.093***	-0.035	0.002	**0.145******	**0.101***
	significance (both sides)		0.001	0.000	0.029	0.411	0.963	0.001	0.018
	N	564	558	549	547	539	543	545	552

*The correlation is significant at a level of 0.05 (both sides)

**The correlation is significant at a level of 0.01 (both sides)

Table 17: Pearson Correlation between General and Informational Social Web Usage. Source: own survey

The strongest correlation between general social web usage and using the social web as an information source exists for social networks ($r = 0.332, p = 0.000$). Next follow travel communities and hotel review sites ($r = 0.145$ resp. $r = 0.14, p < 0.01$). The informational use of booking sites with review function and media sharing platforms is also positively correlated with the general social web usage ($r = 0.101$ resp. $r = 0.093, p < 0.05$) . The correlation coefficients for microblogs and blogs & podcasts are tending towards zero and no correlation is assumed.

The analyses show that the informational use of hotel review sites, social networks, media sharing platforms, travel communities and booking sites with review function depends on the general frequency of social web use: with growing general social web usage these sites are accessed more often during the information search. This effect is especially strong for social networks.

It has been additionally tested if differences between genders arise. The only significant difference can be found for hotel review sites, which are used as a source of information a little more often by women than by men (mean = 1.8 resp. 1.9). The difference is significant according to the t-test ($p < 0.05$) and the ANOVA ($p < 0.05$). The Pearson correlation presents a coefficient of $r = -0.111$ at the significant level of $p < 0.05$. As women do neither have a higher travel frequency nor distinctly access hotel review sites more often, the difference is noteworthy. The age is not considered in RH I, as RH II is dedicated to the analysis of age.

6.3.1.2 Discussion of Research Hypothesis I

The purpose of RH I was to determine whether the informational use of the social web is dependent on the user characteristics regarding travel frequency and general social web usage. The aim was to make characteristics of social information seekers more transparent in order to identify the type of users who can be reached on the social web.

Regarding general social web usage, RH I demonstrated that hotel review sites, social networks, media sharing platforms, travel communities and booking sites with review function are more often accessed as a source of information by frequent than by occasional social web users. The difference is especially distinct for social networks. This can be explained due to the fact that social networks can be considered as a source of information by active social network users only: users need a personal login and a profile, which is mostly created only if users intend to use the site on a regular basis. This is also valid for travel communities, where personal involvement is mostly existent. However, it is important to point out that this does not apply to hotel review sites, media sharing platforms and booking sites with review function. These sites neither require a personal profile nor a regular use. Their functionality and navigation is rather self-explaining and requires no previous experience. Summarizing, it can be said that mostly, frequent social web users consider social web sites during their information search. The implications for hotels is that only a certain subset of the guest mix can be reached on the social web. Hence, a significant percentage – namely those guests who use the social web rarely or not at all – is mostly not affected by the possibilities the social web offers regarding information search.

Considering the impact of the travel frequency on the degree of informational social web usage, only differences for hotel review sites and booking sites with review function could be detected. Both are more often accessed during the information process by frequent travellers. All other sites are considered equally by frequent and occasional hotel guests, therefore the corporate social web communication may approach both target groups.

RH I identified hotel review sites and booking sites with review function as the most important source of information on the social web. The importance of social networks, travel communities and media sharing platforms was also shown, however, it is currently rather limited. Only a small share of guests consider these sites as an information source. Additionally, an important finding of RH I is the general insignificance of blogs & podcasts and microblogs. All the conducted analyses showed that none of these social web sites play a role during the information search but are mostly neglected. This insignificance is an important result: it is observed that many hotels – in addition to their communication on Facebook – send daily tweets via the microblogging service Twitter. Twitter is obviously perceived as a popular corporate communication channel – however, as the findings of RH I demonstrate Twitter is not considered during the information search. Hoteliers should therefore strongly question whether their financial efforts for communicating in this microblogging service are justified.

As microblogs and blogs & podcasts proved to be irrelevant for the information search, they will be excluded from the following analyses.

6.3.2 Research Hypothesis II

6.3.2.1 Statistical Analysis of Research Hypothesis II

RH II: The informational social web usage differs between the younger generation and best agers.

As was shown in chapter 2, best agers generally use the social web less frequently than younger users. However, the question arises if this automatically implies that best agers do not integrate the social web into their information process. Therefore, both user groups are compared and analyzed. The following paragraphs investigate the information behaviour of best agers compared to users aged 18 to 55 years.

To begin with, the booking method is analyzed to see if there are already distinct differences regarding online and offline bookings:

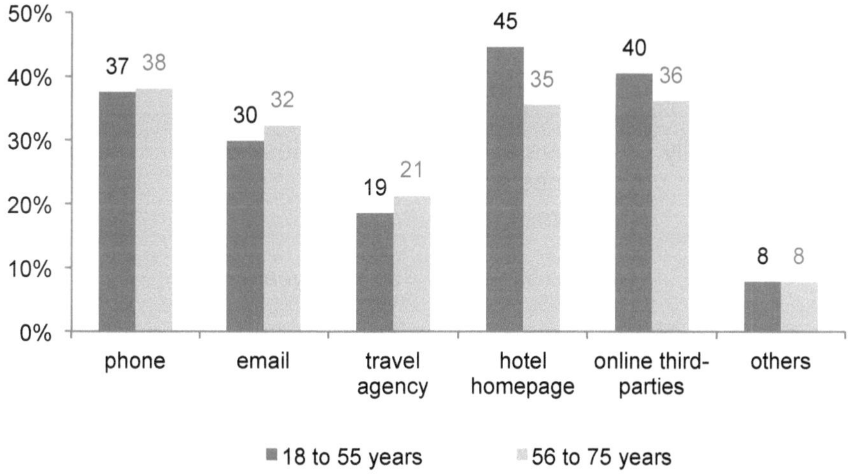

Fig. 32: Booking Method by Age Groups. Multiple responses possible. Source: own survey

While for the younger generation the most important booking method is the hotel homepage, followed by online third-party providers and the phone, best agers see the phone as the most relevant booking method, followed by online third-party providers and the hotel homepage.

Considering the booking method profit relationships addressed in chapter 4, the fact that hotel websites and phone calls are important booking methods for both groups is a positive result. For both age groups, reservations by email and via travel agencies follows next. Considering the booking method, no great differences between the groups can be found, as both age groups acknowledge the importance of online bookings.

The consideration of the general Internet usage does not reveal significant differences between the age groups either.

The following diagram presents the general social web usage of both age groups:

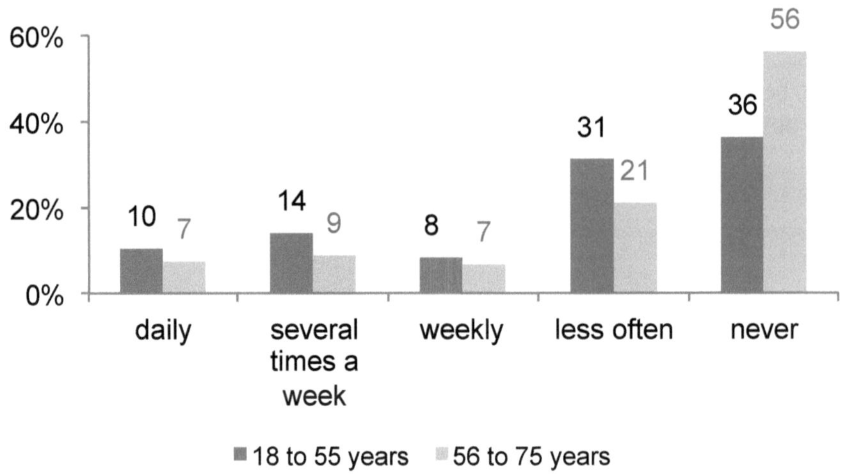

Fig. 33: Social Web Usage by Age Groups. Source: own survey

The diagram shows that there are relatively no distinct differences in the daily and weekly usage between both age groups. There is a difference of five percent points of users who access the social web several times a week in favour of the younger age group. The biggest difference can be found between users who do not use the social web at all, with 20 percent points more best agers reporting that they never access it.

Regarding online and offline information channels, there are no distinct differences: for all participants the Internet is by far the most important information source. Travel agencies and brochures are named second most important, followed by friends and family. Regarding the online information sources no distinct differences arise either.

The following diagram depicts the informational use of social web sites by both age groups:

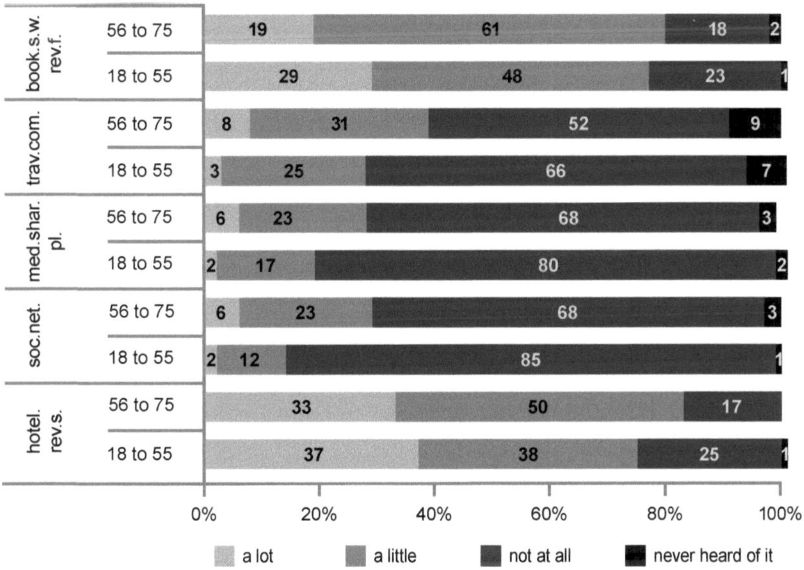

Fig. 34: Informational Use of Social Web Sites by Age Groups. Source: own survey

As can be seen, hotel review sites and booking sites with review function are the most important social web sites for both age groups. The third and fourth most important applications are travel communities and social networks, finally followed by media sharing platforms. Without exception, all sites are – relatively seen – used as an information source more intensively by best agers than by younger users.

The information subjects of most interest are the same for both age groups: rooms, location and service.

Personal reviews are shared mainly on hotel review sites and booking sites with review function. With a great gap travel communities and social networks follow. The sharing of photos and videos on media sharing platforms is rather seldom.

The following diagram presents the reporting (frequent and occasional) by age groups:

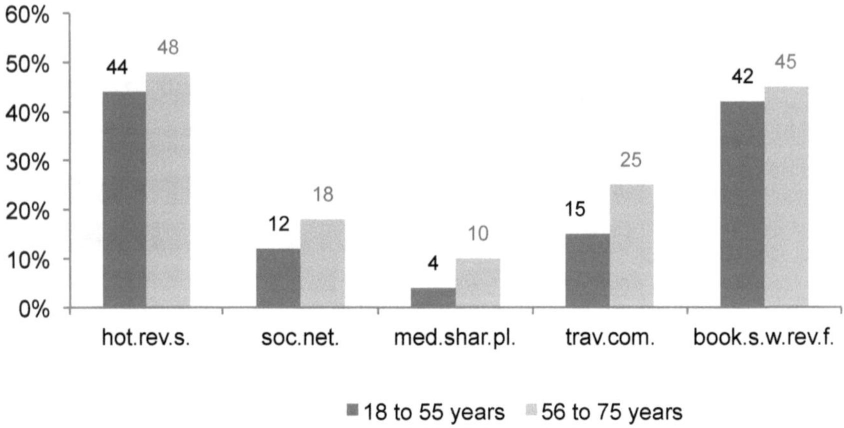

Fig. 35: Reporting by Age Groups. Source: own survey

The older generation is more active than younger users, especially on travel communities, where 25% of all the considered guests between 56 and 75 share reviews and experiences.

The frequency distribution has revealed interesting findings. There are best agers who are as equally active on the social web as the younger generation, relatively seen even exceeding them. Concluding from the frequency distribution, best agers may also be reached on the social web. The following paragraphs analyze the statistical relevance of the social information behaviour of best agers, compared to that of the younger generation.

According to the chi-square test, there is a significant relationship between age and the informational use of social networks ($p < 0.05$). The following table presents the means[446] of the age groups 18 to 55 and 56 to 75 regarding informational use of the different social web sites:

446 The means may range from 1 to 4 (1 = used a lot, 2 = used a little, 3 = not used at all, 4 = never heard of it).

age		hot.rev.s.	soc.net.	med.shar.plat.	tr.comm.	book.s.w.rev.
18 to 55	mean	**1.90**	**2.84**	**2.82**	**2.76**	**1.96**
	N	459	451	449	449	455
	st. dev.	0.807	0.455	0.470	0.611	0.741
56 to 75	mean	**1.84**	**2.68**	**2.74**	**2.63**	**2.01**
	N	70	66	66	65	67
	st. dev.	0.694	0.636	0.590	0.762	0.663
total	mean	**1.89**	**2.82**	**2.81**	**2.74**	**1.96**
	N	529	517	515	514	522
	st. dev.	0.793	0.484	0.487	0.632	0.731

Table 18: Means: Social Web Usage by Age Groups. Source: own survey

With the exception of booking sites with review function, best agers integrate the displayed social web sites more often into their information process than the younger generation does. The difference in means is especially noteworthy for social networks (mean = 2.68 resp. 2.84). The following diagram presents the calculated means graphically:

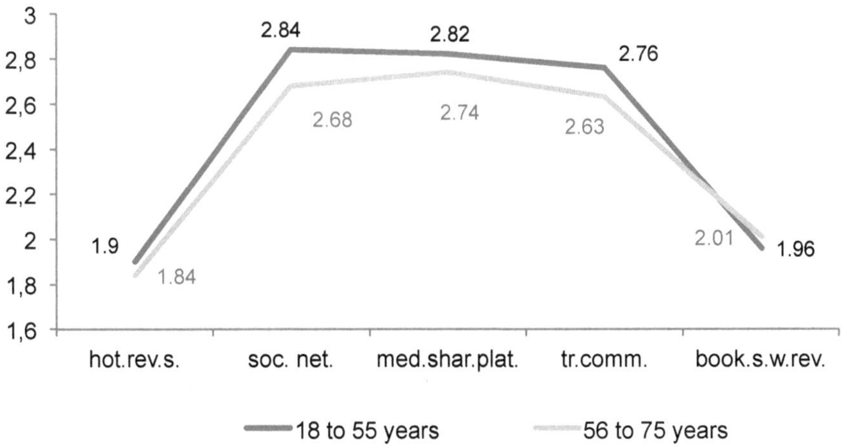

Fig. 36: Means: Informational Social Web Usage by Age Groups. Source: own survey

As can be clearly seen, the means of the older generation are equivalent to or lower than the means of the younger generation, thereby indicating a more intensive usage. The t-test confirms a significant difference for social networks ($p < 0.05$), as does the ANOVA ($p < 0.05$). Also, the ANCOVA states that the covariate age has a significant relationship with the informational use of social networks ($p < 0.05$). However, as R Squared reaches the value of 0.013, tending towards zero, it may not be suitable to predict differences.

The following table presents the correlation analysis:[447]

		age	hot.rev.s.	soc.net.	med.shar.plat.	tr.comm.	book.s.w.rev.
age	correlation after Pearson	1	0.025	**0.112***	0.051	0.065	-0.027
	significance (both sides)		0.562	0.011	0.244	0.139	0.539
	N	862	529	517	515	514	522

*The correlation is significant at a level of 0.05 (both sides)

Table 19: Pearson Correlation between Age and Informational Social Web Usage. Source: own survey

There is a significant relationship between age and the informational use of social networks with $r = 0.112$ ($p < 0.05$), stating that the use slightly increases with growing age. The correlation coefficients of the other sites are tending towards zero and hence no relationship can be defined.

6.3.2.2 Discussion of Research Hypothesis II

The aim of RH II was to analyze whether there is a significant difference between the younger generation and best agers regarding their informational social web usage.

Chapter 2 presented the different types of online users, namely digital natives, digital immigrants and digital outsiders. As best agers were not born into the digital world, it is easy to assume that they are digital outsiders. However, the calcu-

447 Since both of the variables considered have to run into the same direction from positive to negative resp. high to low, the variable age was recoded.

lated results of RH II show that *some* best agers rather should be regarded as digital immigrants.

The consideration of the frequency distribution stated that younger users and best agers access the Internet rather to the same extent. However, looking at their social web usage, differences become apparent. The younger age group generally accesses the social web more intensively than best agers. Additionally, there are many more Internet users aged older than 55 years who do not use the social web at all. However, the differences in usage diminish when the informational social web usage is considered. It was interesting to learn that best agers and younger users access the social web as a source of information to the same extent. The statistics presented no significant differences in the informational use of the social web. The only exception were social networks, which are more often used by best agers. Generally, certain best agers consider the social web as an information source as equally as the younger generation does, sometimes even exceeding them: additionally and relatively seen, best agers publish more reviews and contribute more content, especially on travel communities. Hence, best agers may also significantly influence the booking decision of other users by sharing their reviews.

Most certainly, it must be acknowledged that the total number of best agers already using the social web as a source of information is by far smaller than the number of younger users. Therefore, the validity of the findings has to be considered carefully. Nevertheless, the assumption that best agers do not use the social web as a source of information can be categorically rejected.

Regarding the corporate communication strategy, these results imply that best agers can also be reached on the social web. As presented in the section of chapter 2 dealing with online development over the last years, the number of best agers using the Internet in general and the social web in particular has considerably increased within recent years. With usage expected to grow even further in the future, the number of best agers using the social web to also gather information is predicted to increase proportionately. Hence, a positive development for the social web's importance for best agers may be predicted. As best agers mostly have both financial resources and time to travel, they present an interesting target group for hotels. From a hotel's standpoint, it seems to be beneficial to engage with best agers on the social web.

6.3.3 Research Hypothesis III

6.3.3.1 Statistical Analysis of Research Hypothesis III

RH III: The varying social web sites have a different impact on the personal hotel booking decision.

RH III presumes that the impact of the social web on the personal booking decision cannot be generalized but has to be considered separately for the different types of social web applications. While it is assumed that reviews and comments on certain sites have a significant impact on the personal booking decision, others may be insignificant and do not influence the booking decision.

Already 27.1% of the considered participants have changed an existing booking decision due to negative reviews on the social web. For hotels, it is hence important to be aware of the different impacts in order to observe contents on the relevant sites.

At first, the means[448] of the impact of the different sites are calculated in order to get a general impression of the impact:

	hot.rev.s.	**soc.net.**	**med.shar.plat.**	**tr.comm.**	**book.s.w.rev.**
mean	**1.61**	**2.50**	**2.62**	**2.42**	**1.75**
N	571	554	552	549	559
st. dev.	0.705	0.712	0.654	0.826	0.740

Table 20: Means: Impact of the Social Web Sites on the Booking Decision. Source: own survey

Hotel review sites have the highest impact on the personal booking decision with a mean of 1.61, followed by booking sites with review function that have a mean of 1.75. The next higher means can be found for travel communities (mean = 2.42) and social networks (mean = 2.5), however, the means of travel communities and social networks are significantly higher, hence their impact on the booking decision is correspondingly lower. Media sharing platforms reach a mean of 2.62. According to the means, hotel review sites and booking sites with review function

448 The means may range from 1 to 4 (1 = high impact, 2 = some impact, 3 = few impact, 4 = never heard of it).

have a rather high impact on the booking decision while some influence can be detected for travel communities, social networks and media sharing platforms.

Hotel review sites, booking sites with review function and with limitations also travel communities, social networks and media sharing platforms have been acknowledged as providing influencing content for the booking decision. The question arises if there are users who are more influenced than others and if so, which characteristics they have. Therefore, the following paragraphs will investigate the demographics gender and age as well as the characteristics travel frequency and general social web usage.

Gender

The first assumption is that the dimension of the impact may depend on gender. Possibly, women can be influenced more easily than men or vice versa.

According to the chi-square test, there is a significant relation between genders and the informational use of hotel review sites, social networks and travel communities ($p < 0.05$). The following diagram presents the different means[449] by gender:

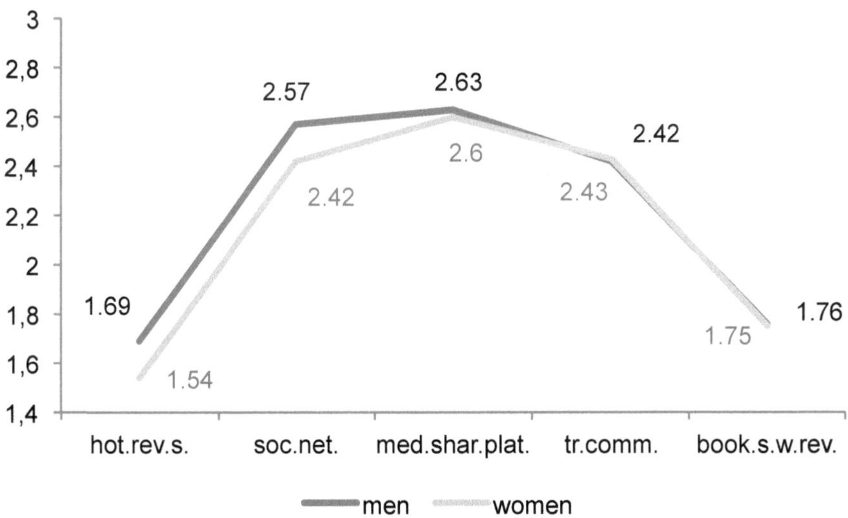

Fig. 37: Means: Impact of the Social Web Sites by Gender. Source: own survey

449 The means may range from 1 to 4 (1 = high impact, 2 = some impact, 3 = few impact, 4 = never heard of it).

The diagram shows that reviews on hotel review sites and social networks have a higher influence on female users (mean = 1.54 resp. 2.42) than on males (mean = 1.69 resp. 2.57). For all other sites no distinct differences exist. The differences for hotel review sites and social networks are significant according to the t-test ($p < 0.05$). The ANOVA confirms an effect of the gender on the informational use of hotel review sites and social networks ($p < 0.05$). This is also supported by the ANCOVA ($p < 0.05$). However, as the values of R Squared amount to 0.013 for hotel review sites and 0.007 for social networks, they are not suitable for the prediction of differences.

In order to verify the results of the previous calculations, a correlation analysis has been performed. The results are as follows:

		gender	hot.rev.s.	soc.net.	med.shar.plat.	tr.comm.	book.s.w.rev.
gender	correlation after Pearson	1.000	**-0.105***	**-0.104***	-0.022	0.003	-0.009
	significance (both sides)		0.013	0.015	0.606	0.949	0.830
	N	907	562	545	543	540	551

*The correlation is significant at a level of 0.05 (both sides)

Table 21: Pearson Correlation between Genders and Impact of the Social Web. Source: own survey

The correlation coefficient of hotel review sites ($r = -0.105$) and social networks ($r = -0.104$) is significant ($p < 0.05$) and supports the previous finding that the impact of these sites differs with regard to gender. For none of the other sites a correlation could be detected. Hence, women are slightly more easily influenced by reviews on hotel review sites and social networks than men.

Age

As it may be possible that older guests are more decisively influenced by reviews on the social web than younger users (or vice versa), the following analyses will examine if there are differences in the influence by age groups.

The chi-square test shows a significant relation between age and the influence of social networks ($p < 0.05$). The following figure presents the different means:[450]

450 The means may range from 1 to 4 (1 = high impact, 2 = some impact, 3 = few impact, 4 = never heard of it).

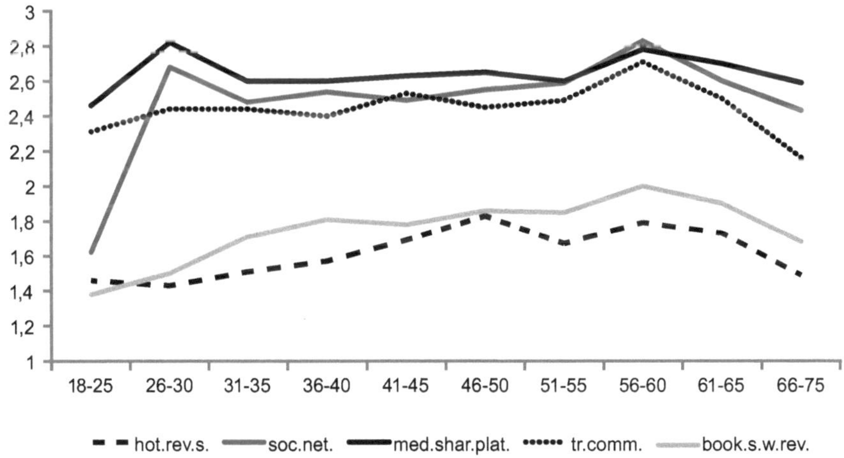

Fig. 38: Means: Impact of the Social Web Sites by Age[451]. Source: own survey

As the diagram clearly shows, the impact of social networks, media sharing platforms and travel communities is generally much lower than the influence of hotel review sites and booking sites with review function. Although no general trend can be identified, there are some differences between age groups: hotel review sites have an above-average influence on users aged 18 to 30 while they are substandard important to users aged 46 to 50. Booking sites show a similar influence. Social networks have an above-average impact on the age group 18 to 25. The age groups 61 to 75 and 18 to 25 are influenced to a greater extent by reviews on travel communities. The observation of the means presents different impacts for the various age groups. However, since these differences seem random in nature, no clear statement regarding the group differences can be made. This is also supported by the performed t-test, which presents no significant differences between the age groups for any of the sites ($p > 0.05$).[452] The conducted ANOVA shows the only significant age-specific influence to be social networks ($p < 0.05$). The ANCOVA does not present a significant relationship between the covariate age and the impact of the social web sites ($p > 0.05$).

451 For reasons of clarity the different means are not displayed.

452 For the independent t-test younger users were defined as representing the age 18 to 55 while older users were defined as having the age 56 to 75.

The absence of a correlation between age and impact is further confirmed by the correlation analysis:[453]

		age	hot.rev.s.	soc. net.	med.shar.plat.	tr.comm.	book.s.w.rev.
age	correlation after Pearson	1.000	0.036	-0.048	-0.040	-0.052	0.070
	significance (both sides)		0.415	0.275	0.361	0.239	0.112
	N	917	529	517	515	514	522

Table 22: Pearson Correlation between Age and Impact of the Social Web. Source: own survey

All correlation coefficients are tending towards zero ($p > 0.05$) and no correlation can be determined.

In general, no distinct differences between the age groups and the impact of the social web on the personal booking decision can be determined.

Travel Frequency

The impact of reviews on social web sites may depend on travel frequency: frequent hotel guests may have had good or bad experiences with the quality of reviews, therefore perhaps being more influenced by them than occasional hotel guests.

According to the chi-square test, no relationship between travel frequency and the degree of impact exists ($p > 0.05$). The following diagram shows the means[454] of the impact by travel frequency.

453 Since both of the variables considered have to run into the same direction from positive to negative resp. high to low, the variable age was recoded.

454 The means may range from 1 to 4 (1 = high impact, 2 = some impact, 3 = few impact, 4 = never heard of it).

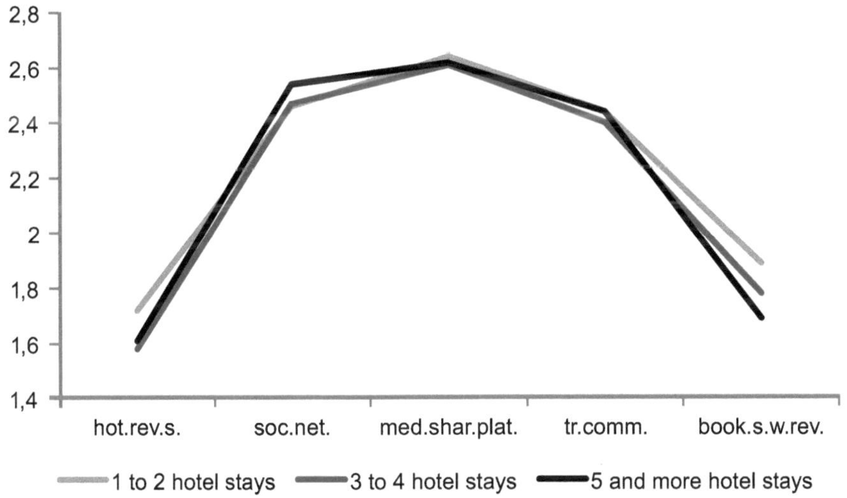

Fig. 39: Means: Impact of the Social Web Sites by Travel Frequency[455]. Source: own survey

The means of some sites reveal differences in impact. Booking sites with review function differ with travel frequency: frequent travellers are more influenced by them than occasional travellers (mean = 1.69 resp. 1.89). To a lesser extent, this also applies to social networks (mean = 2.46 resp. 2.54) and hotel review sites (mean = 1.61 resp. 1.72). The t-test[456] does not state significant differences ($p > 0.05$). The ANOVA confirms that there is a significant effect of the travel frequency on the influence of reviews on booking sites ($p < 0.05$). According to the ANCOVA, the covariate travel frequency has a significant relationship with the informational use of booking sites with review function ($p < 0.05$). However, the R Squared is tending to zero, therefore it may not be used for prediction.

The correlation analysis[457] reveals a significant correlation coefficient for booking sites with review function.

455 For reasons of clarity the different means are not displayed.

456 For the independent t-test occasional travellers were defined as having 1 to 2 hotel stays per year while frequent travellers were defined as having 3 and more hotel stays per year.

457 Since both of the variables considered have to run into the same direction from positive to negative resp. high to low, the variable travel frequency was recoded.

		travel frequency	hot.rev.s.	soc. net.	med.shar.plat.	tr.comm.	book.s.w.rev.
travel frequency	correlation after Pearson	1.000	0.035	-0.048	0.005	-0.009	**0.098***
	significance (both sides)		0.404	0.257	0.899	0.839	0.021
	N	924	569	553	551	548	557

*The correlation is significant at a level of 0.05 (both sides)

Table 23: Pearson Correlation between Travel Frequency and Impact of the Social Web. Source: own survey

The correlation coefficient of booking sites with review function is significant ($r = 0.098$, $p < 0.05$) and states that there exists a slight correlation between travel frequency and the impact of booking sites with review function. The correlation coefficients of all other sites are tending towards zero and no correlation can be assumed. With the exception of booking sites, frequent and occasional travellers are influenced by reviews on social web sites to the same extent. As booking sites with review function do not only provide information but also booking possibilities, frequent travellers may access them more often, thereby possibly being more exposed to reviews and more influenced by them.

General Social Web Usage

Lastly, the general social web usage is analyzed to see if the degree of the reviews' impact depends on the general social web usage. As frequent social web users may be exposed more often to reviews, they are possibly also more influenced by them. The chi-square test states that there is a significant relation between the degree of the general social web usage and the impact of reviews on social networks and travel communities ($p < 0.05$). The following table presents the means[458] of the different sites' impact by the general social web usage.

458 The means may range from 1 to 4 (1 = high impact, 2 = some impact, 3 = few impact, 4 = never heard of it).

frequency of using the social web		hot.rev.s.	soc.net.	med.shar.plat.	tr.comm.	book.s.w.rev.
daily	mean	**1.55**	**2.22**	**2.59**	**2.30**	**1.74**
	N	94	92	91	91	94
	st. dev.	0.682	0.782	0.614	0.863	0.842
several times a week	mean	**1.42**	**2.37**	**2.55**	**2.33**	**1.63**
	N	123	121	119	117	121
	st. dev.	0.627	0.685	0.660	0.830	0.660
weekly	mean	**1.64**	**2.60**	**2.62**	**2.39**	**1.77**
	N	76	73	74	75	74
	st. dev.	0.687	0.640	0.656	0.787	0.732
less often	mean	**1.71**	**2.65**	**2.69**	**2.54**	**1.81**
	N	255	246	246	245	249
	st. dev.	0.718	0.677	0.648	0.812	0.724
total	mean	1.61	2.50	2.63	2.43	1.75
	N	548	532	530	528	538
	st. dev.	0.696	0.712	0.647	0.826	0.735

Table 24: Means: Impact of the Social Web by General Social Web Usage. Source: own survey

As the table shows, all means of daily social web users are lower than the means of less-than-weekly users, thereby indicating that frequent social web users are more influenced by reviews. The differences in means are especially noteworthy for hotel review sites (mean = 1.55 resp. 1.71), social networks (mean = 2.22 resp. 2.65) and travel communities (mean = 2.3 resp. 2.54). The t-test[459] determines a significant difference for these three sites ($p < 0.05$), as does the ANOVA ($p < 0.05$). The ANCOVA shows that the covariate general social web usage has a significant relationship with the impact of hotel review sites, social networks, media sharing platforms and travel communities ($p < 0.05$):

459 For the independent t-test frequent social web users are defined as using the social web at least weekly, while occasional users are defined as using it less often.

source		type III sum of square	df	mean square	F	sig.
corrected model	hot.rev.s.	4.413[a]	1	4.413	9.099	**0.003**
	soc.net.	14.376[b]	1	14.376	29.831	**0.000**
	med.shar.plat.	1.674[c]	1	1.674	4.149	**0.042**
	trav.comm.	5.391[d]	1	5.391	8.020	**0.005**
	book.s.w.rev.	1.198[e]	1	1.198	2.215	0.137
a. R Squared = 0.018 (adjusted R Squared = 0.016)						
b. R Squared = 0.055 (adjusted R Squared = 0.054)						
c. R Squared = 0.008 (adjusted R Squared = 0.006)						
d. R Squared = 0.016 (adjusted R Squared = 0.014)						
e. R Squared = 0.004 (adjusted R Squared = 0.002)						

Table 25: Test of Between-Subjects Effects: Impact of Social Web Sites by General Social Web Usage. Source: own survey

As the values of R Squared are tending towards zero, the variables may not be predictable.

Lastly, a correlation analysis has been conducted:

		social web usage	hot.rev.s.	soc.net.	med.shar.plat.	tr.comm.	book.s.w.rev.
social web usage	correlation after Pearson	1.000	**0.130***	**0.234***	0.074	**0.124***	0.067
	significance (both sides)		0.002	0.000	0.087	0.004	0.119
	N	564	548	532	530	528	538
*The correlation is significant at a level of 0.01 (both sides)							

Table 26: Pearson Correlation between General Social Web Usage and Impact of the Social Web. Source: own survey

The correlation analysis shows that the general social web usage is significantly related to the impact of reviews on social networks ($r = 0.234$), on hotel review sites ($r = 0.130$) and on travel communities ($r = 0.124$), $p < 0.01$.

Summing up, it can be stated that frequent social web users are more influenced by reviews on hotel review sites, social networks and travel communities than occasional social web users.

6.3.3.2 Discussion of Research Hypothesis III

The aim of RH III was to define the general impact of the social web's different sites as well as to examine if certain user characteristics are decisive for the degree of impact.

Of all the considered participants, 27.1% have already withdrawn their existing booking decision due to negative reviews. This is a large number, which shows that negative reviews may severely impact the guest's booking decision. Generally, the biggest impact on the personal booking decision could be attributed to reviews on hotel review sites. Booking sites with review function were also identified as an influencing channel. The impact of reviews and comments on travel communities, social networks and media sharing platforms could also be detected, however, their influence is significantly lower. It was expected that hotel review sites have the biggest impact on the personal booking decision, as users easily find a great number of reviews, averagely presenting a reliable general picture. Hotel review sites thereby present an adequate decision support. As this also accounts for booking sites with review function, they were consequently named second most important.

Reviews on hotel review sites and on social networks have a slightly higher influence on women than on men while all other sites are equally important to both genders. Between the different age groups no noteworthy differences could be detected. With the exception of booking sites, the degree of impact does not correlate with the travel frequency. Regarding general social web usage, frequent social web users are more impacted by reviews on hotel review sites, social networks and travel communities than occasional users.

For hotels the conducted analyses present important findings as they prove that reviews have a significant impact on the booking decision of guests. Additionally, RH III showed that while hotel review sites and booking sites with review function have the highest impact, also social networks, media sharing platforms and travel communities may influence the booking decision. It is therefore of utmost importance to observe not only the popular review sites but also social networks, media sharing platforms and travel communities. Monitoring tools, which were presented in chapter 2, may help to gain an overview of the ever increasing mass of reviews. Hotels should undertake any efforts to elevate positive reviews as well as to comment on negative reports, as they may severely impact the booking decision of future guests.

6.3.4 Research Hypothesis IV

6.3.4.1 Statistical Analysis of Research Hypothesis IV

RH IV: The social web has the potential to evolve into a relevant distribution channel.

The aim of RH IV is to find out whether the social web is perceived by users as a communication and information channel only, or if it can develop into a distribution channel in the future. While hotel review sites formerly were pure review sites, today – almost without exception – booking possibilities are integrated. Hotels also start to incorporate the possibility of booking a hotel room on social networks. However, the question arises if the social web is appreciated as a distribution channel, as it was initially developed in order to boost communication and interaction.

Of all the considered participants 26.9% confirm that they would book their hotel room directly on the social web while 73.1% claimed they would not.

The most immediate assumption is that the bias for or against social bookings depends on the dimension the social web is used generally and specifically as an information source.

Therefore, the first variable analyzed is general social web usage. The chi-square test shows no significant relationship between general social web usage and social bookings affinity ($p > 0.05$). The consideration of the means[460] reveal that daily social web users (mean = 1.66) are a little more open to the possibility of social bookings than less than weekly users (mean = 1.77).[461] The difference is not significant according to the t-test ($p > 0.05$). The ANOVA shows no significant effect of the frequency of social web use to the affinity of social bookings either ($p > 0.05$), neither does the univariate ANCOVA ($p > 0.05$). The correlation analysis

460 The means refer to the question: 'Would you also book your hotel room on the social web?' and may range from 1 = yes to 2 = no.

461 The means refer to the question: 'Would you also book your hotel room on the social web?' and may range from 1 = yes to 2 = no.

states that there is no significant relationship between general use of the social web and the attitude towards social bookings ($r = 0.075, p > 0.05$).

However, when examining the degree of the informational social web usage, the picture changes. The chi-square test shows a significant relationship between the informational use of all considered social web sites and the attitude towards social bookings ($p < 0.05$).

The following diagram presents the means[462] of the booking affinity, differentiated by the usage of the social web sites as an information source:

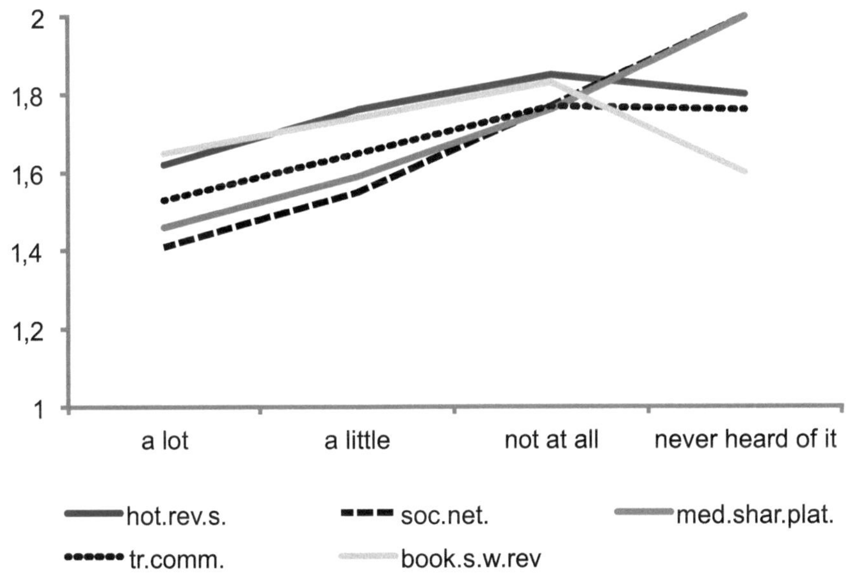

Fig. 40: Means: Social Bookings Affinity by Informational Social Web Usage[463]. Source: own survey

As can be seen, the graphs rise with decreasing informational use, indicating that guests who use the social web as an information source are more open to the possibility of social bookings than those who do not access social web sites during their information gathering.

462 The means refer to the question: 'Would you also book your hotel room on the social web?' and may range from 1 = yes to 2 = no.

463 For reasons of clarity the means are not displayed.

The means show significant differences for social networks in particular: users who access social networks a lot as a source of information reach a mean of 1.41 while users who do not use social networks reach a mean of 1.77. The means of media sharing platforms (mean = 1.46 resp. 1.76), travel communities (mean = 1.53 resp. 1.77), hotel review sites (mean = 1.62 resp. 1.85) and booking sites with review function (mean = 1.65 resp. 1.83) are also lower for users who consider these sites as a source of information. According to the t-test,[464] the differences are significant for all sites ($p < 0.05$). The ANOVA confirms a significant effect of the informational social web usage of all sites on the attitude towards social bookings ($p < 0.05$).[465] The ANOVA was followed up by a discriminant analysis. According to the test of consistency, which evaluates the model's quality, the differences for all social web sites are significant ($p < 0.01$).

	Wilks-Lambda	**F**	**df1**	**df2**	**significance**
hot.rev.s.	0.961	22.067	1	540	**0.000**
soc.net.	0.952	27.397	1	540	**0.000**
med.shar.plat.	0.971	16.395	1	540	**0.000**
trav.com.	0.985	8.29	1	540	**0.004**
book.s.w.rev.	0.978	11.872	1	540	**0.001**

Table 27: Test of Consistency of the Group Means: Social Bookings Affinity and Informational Social Web Usage. Source: own survey

The first function explains 100% of the model and the following standardized canonical discriminant function coefficients arise:

464 For the independent t-test the participants were divided into users who use the social web as an information source and those who do not.

465 The ANOVA has been carried out separately for the different social web sites.

	function 1
hot.rev.s.	**0.442**
soc.net	**0.517**
med.shar.plat.	0.292
tr.comm.	**0.007**
book.s.w.rev.	0.166

Table 28: St.Can.Dis.Fun.Coefficient: Social Bookings Affinity and Informational Social Web Usage. Source: own survey

As can be seen, social networks and hotel review sites have the highest importance while travel communities the least. As Wilks' Lambda of the first function is highly significant ($p = 0.000$) it can be stated that the attitude towards social bookings can be explained by the informational use of the social web sites. The consideration of the cross table shows that 62.8% of users with a positive view and 63.5% of users with a negative view towards social bookings can be predicted, hence the quality of the model is judged positively.[466] Also, *phi* is significant ($p < 0.05$).

The correlation analysis states significant relationships between the use of the social web as an information source and the perception of social bookings:

		social bookings affinity	hot.rev.s.	soc.net.	med.shar.plat.	tr.comm.	book.s.w.rev.
social bookings affinity	correlation after Pearson	1.000	**0.196***	**0.222***	**0.186***	**0.131***	**0.134***
	significance (both sides)		0.000	0.000	0.000	0.002	0.001
	N	583	575	563	562	559	568

*The correlation is significant at a level of 0.01 (both sides).

Table 29: Pearson Correlation between Social Bookings Affinity and Informational Social Web Usage. Source: own survey

The informational use of social networks ($r = 0.222$), hotel review sites ($r = 0.196$), media sharing platforms ($r = 0.186$), booking sites with review function ($r = 0.134$)

466 The complete table 'Expected Cross Tabulation: Social Bookings Affinity and Informational Social Web Usage' can be found in the appendix.

and travel communities ($r = 0.131$) is significantly related to how guests perceive social bookings on the social web ($p < 0.01$): with increasing informational use of these sites, the attitude towards social bookings becomes more positive.

The conducted analyses confirm a relationship between social bookings affinity and informational usage of the social web. It can therefore be stated that the possibility of booking a hotel room on the social web is more appealing to users who use the social web as an information source.

No relationship can be determined with regards to age. The means differ between age groups but no clear trend can be defined. The t-test shows no significant difference between the age groups ($p > 0.05$). The ANOVA also states that there is no significant effect of age on the perception of social bookings ($p > 0.05$).[467] The correlation analysis does not detect any relationship between age and social bookings affinity ($r = -0.004, p > 0.05$). Summing up, the bias for or against social bookings does not depend on age. There is no difference with regard to gender either. Neither can a difference be determined regarding travel frequency.

6.3.4.2 Discussion of Research Hypothesis IV

The aim of RH IV was to judge whether the possibility of social bookings is accepted as a booking method or if it is rather rejected by users.

About one quarter of all relevant participants answered that they would book their hotel room on the social web. Although this number seems to be rather small at first glance, it gains in significance when considering certain aspects. As chapter 2 showed, the Internet and social web usage has been constantly increasing within the last few years and will most likely grow even further in the future. It can therefore be assumed that the social web will become an even more integrated part of people's daily lives. This in return will most likely increase online purchasing processes. Additionally, chapter 4 established that the majority of all hotel bookings is already made online. This proves that hotel guests generally have a high affinity to online bookings. The expansion of online bookings to the social web should therefore be feasible. Considering these circumstances, it can be assumed that social bookings will gain in acceptance.

The conducted analyses revealed that the current acceptance of social bookings is higher for users who consider social web sites as a source of information. The implications of this determination are important for the hotel industry. Users who are actively looking for hotel information most probably also need to book a hotel room. Hotels may hence 'catch' those users during their information search

467 The ANOVA has been carried out separately for the different social web sites.

and guide them to the direct social bookings possibility.[468] As the analyses were especially significant for social networks, a booking widget on the hotel's social network fan page (mostly Facebook) seems to be recommendable.

The users were also analyzed with regard to their differing travel frequencies, their ages and their genders. However, none of these factors resulted in significant differences. This is also an important finding, as it states that occasional and frequent travellers, men and women, younger and older users rather have the same view on social bookings. This implies that theoretically, all target groups – who are active on the social web – are willing to conduct social bookings. This represents great potential for this new distribution channel *in the future*.

However, looking back on the number of participants who would *currently* book the hotel room on the social web, it becomes apparent that the current acceptance of social bookings is rather low. Only 26.9% would make a hotel booking on the social web. Hence, at the moment social bookings do not seem to be a popular booking method.

6.3.5 Research Hypothesis V

6.3.5.1 Statistical Analysis of Research Hypothesis V

RH V: The perception of social advertising depends on particular user characteristics.

In addition to the possibility of social bookings, the placing of advertisements on social web sites – social advertising – is becoming more and more popular for hotels.[469] However, social advertising is mostly connected with high costs: an ad banner on Facebook may cost between 0.20 € and 0.30 €[470] per 1,000 displays.[471] The previously presented argumentation for or against social bookings also holds true for social advertising: the social web is mainly a place for social interaction and online social gathering, therefore advertisements for products and services may be perceived negatively. However, consumers purchasing products with a high per-

468 As it was presented in chapter 4, the direct booking is connected with the fewest charges, hence direct social bookings present an attractive possibility for hotels.

469 Exemplary ads can be found in the appendix.

470 Cf. Facebook-werbung.com 2010-2012

471 There are also financing models where companies have to pay per click, thereby only paying for users who are interested and forwarded to the advertisement's back links.

sonal involvement, a category the hotel accommodation falls into according to the previous determination, consider advertisements as a source of information.[472] The following calculations analyze how social ads are perceived by users and if there are distinct characteristics for a positive perception.

Of all relevant participants, 28.1% have already clicked on an ad banner. The sample group's perception of social advertising is as follows:

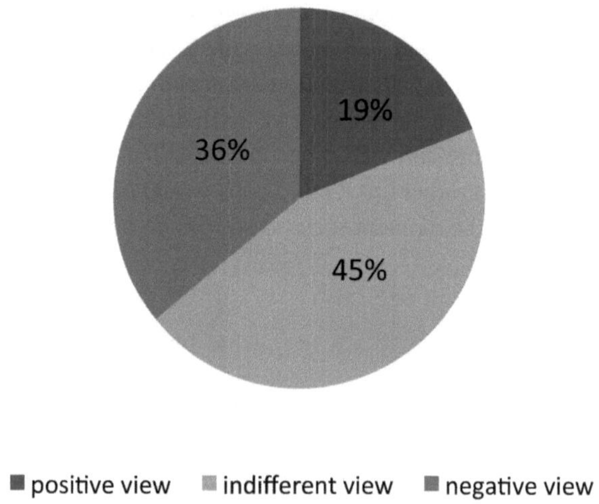

Fig. 41: Perception of Social Advertising. Source: own survey

While the relative majority is indifferent about social advertising, 19% have a positive while 36% have a negative attitude. Hence, 64% have a positive or indifferent view about social advertising.

As it seems fair to suppose that the general social web usage is an important factor for the perception of social advertising, this variable is the first to be examined in the following. It is assumed that frequent social web users are either more accustomed to social advertising and hence have a more positive view or are already bothered by ad banners and therefore have a negative perception.

472 Cf. Kuß et al. 2000, p. 67

According to the chi-square test, there is a significant relation between frequency of social web use and the perception of social advertising ($p = 0.000$). The following figure presents the means[473] by the frequency of use:

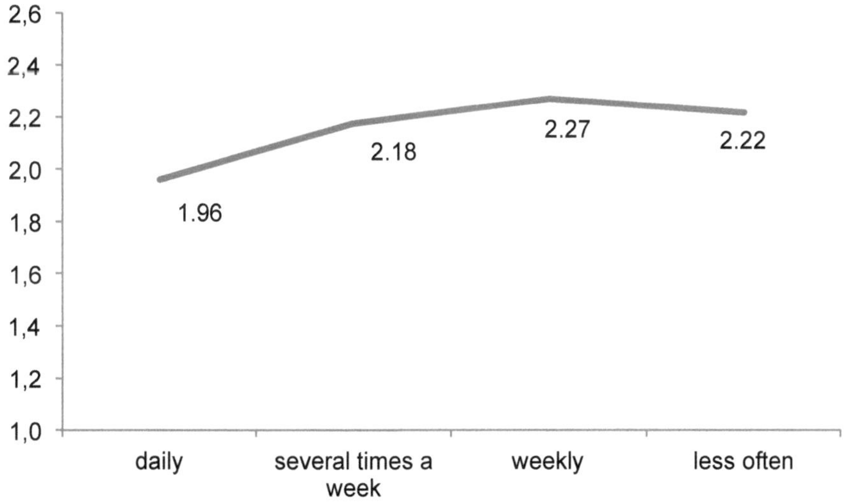

Fig. 42: Means: Attitude towards Social Advertising by General Social Web Usage. Source: own survey

As the diagram shows, daily social web users (mean = 1.96) have a more neutral view than less-than-weekly users (mean = 2.22). The difference is significant according to the t-test ($p < 0.05$). The ANOVA states as well that there is a significant effect of the social web's general usage on the perception of social advertising ($p < 0.05$), as does the univariate ANCOVA ($p < 0.05$).

473 The means may range from 1 to 3 (1 = positive view, 2 = neutral view, 3 = negative view). The data were recoded.

The following table presents the Pearson correlation between the variables.

		perception of social advertising	frequency of using the social web
perception of social advertising	correlation after Pearson	1	**0.112***
	significance (both sides)		0.008
	N	583	558

*The correlation is significant at a level of 0.01 (both sides)

Table 30: Pearson Correlation between Perception of Social Advertising and Frequency of Using the Social Web. Source: own survey

There is a positive correlation ($r = 0.112, p < 0.01$) between frequency of social web use and the perception of advertisements: the more often users access the social web in general, the slightly more positive is their perception of social advertising.

It seems fairly assumable that users who actively search for hotel information on the social web have a positive view on social advertising: as they are in the process of information gathering, ads may provide interesting information. To test this assumption, the next calculations examine informational social web usage.

According to the chi-square test, there is a significant relationship between the degree of informational social web usage and the perception of social advertising ($p < 0.05$ for all sites). The following diagram graphically depicts the means[474] of the perception of social advertising, differentiated by the informational use of the social web sites:

474 The means may range from 1 to 3 (1 = positive view, 2 = neutral view, 3 = negative view). The data were recoded.

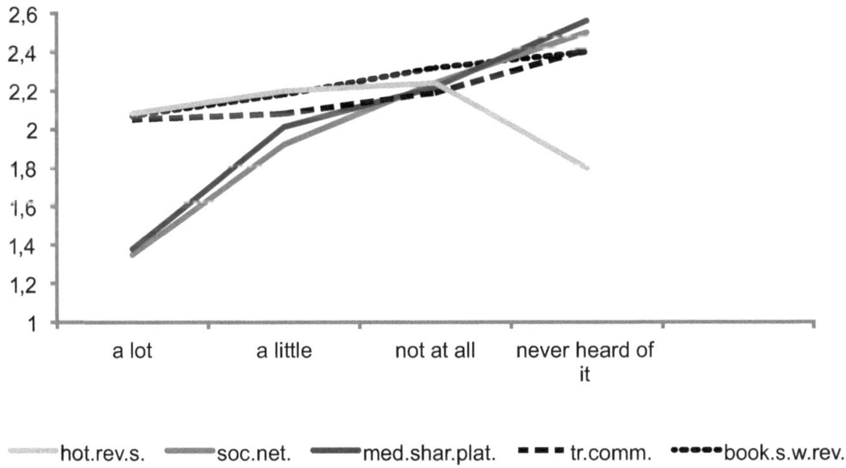

Fig. 43: Means: Attitude towards Social Advertising Perception by Informational Social Web Usage[475]. Source: own survey

As can be seen, users who access social web sites a lot to gather information for their hotel stays have a more positive or neutral attitude towards social advertising than those who use the sites only rarely or not at all. The perception is especially strong for social networks and media sharing platforms, where frequent information gatherer (mean = 1.35 resp. 1.38) clearly have a positive view while users who do not seek for information on these sites (mean = 2.24 resp. 2.22) have a neutral view.[476] Except for hotel review sites and booking sites with review function, the differences are significant according to the t-test[477] ($p < 0.05$). The ANOVA states a significant effect of the degree of informational use of hotel review sites, social networks and media sharing platforms on the perception of social advertising ($p < 0.05$).[478]

475 For reasons of clarity the different means are not displayed.

476 Users who do not know booking sites with review function state an extraordinarily positive perception of social advertising.

477 For the independent t-test the participants were divided into users who use the social web as an information source and those who do not.

478 The ANOVA has been carried out separately for the different social web sites.

Next, a discriminant analysis has been conducted. According to the test of consistency, the differences for hotel review sites, social networks, media sharing platforms and travel communities are significant ($p < 0.01$).

	Wilks-Lambda	F	df1	df2	significance
hot.rev.s.	0.956	12.326	2	538	**0.000**
soc.net.	0.930	20.398	2	538	**0.000**
med.shar.plat.	0.956	12.398	2	538	**0.000**
trav.com.	0.983	4.703	2	538	**0.009**
book.s.w.rev.	0.989	2.937	2	538	0.054

Table 31: Test of Consistency of the Group Means: Perception of Social Advertising and Informational Social Web Usage. Source: own survey

The first function explains 91.3% of the model and the following standardized canonical discriminant function coefficients arise:

	1. function
hot.rev.s.	**0.426**
soc.net	**0.615**
med.shar.plat.	0.350
tr.comm.	0.050
book.s.w.rev.	**-0.063**

Table 32: St.Can.Dis.Fun.Coefficient: Perception of Social Advertising and Informational Social Web Usage. Source: own survey

As can be seen, social networks and hotel review sites have the highest while booking sites with review function have the least importance. As Wilks' Lambda of the first function is highly significant ($p = 0.000$) it can be stated that the perception of social advertising can be explained by the informational use of social web sites. The consideration of the cross table shows that 38.4% of the users with a positive view, 54.1% with a negative and 34.3% with an indifferent view can be predicted with the knowledge of all independent variables.[479] Also, *phi* is significant ($p < 0.05$).

Lastly, a correlation analysis has been conducted to test if there is a significant relationship between the degree of informational social web use and the attitude towards social advertising:

		perception of social advertising	**hot.rev.s.**	**soc. net.**	**med.shar.plat.**	**tr.comm.**	**book.s.w.rev.**
perception of social advertising	correlation after Pearson	1.000	**0.139****	**0.252****	**0.200****	**0.108***	0.066
	significance (both sides)		0.001	0.000	0.000	0.011	0.116
	N	583	575	563	561	559	568

**The correlation is significant at a level of 0.01 (both sides)

*The correlation is significant at a level of 0.05 (both sides)

Table 33: Pearson Correlation between Social Advertising and Informational Social Web Usage. Source: own survey

According to Pearson's correlation coefficients, the informational use of social networks ($r = 0.252$, $p = 0.000$), media sharing platforms ($r = 0.200$, $p = 0.000$), hotel review sites ($r = 0.139$, $p < 0.01$) and travel communities ($r = 0.108$, $p < 0.05$) is significantly related to the perception of social advertising: the more often users seek for information on these sites, the more positive they perceive social advertising.

Regarding travel frequency, the conducted analyses reveal no differences: both frequent and occasional travellers rather have the same attitude towards social advertising. Gender was investigated as well, however, it does not have an impact on the perception of social advertising.

Lastly, the age is considered to test if this variable can explain the attitude towards social advertising. The chi-square test does not state a relationship between

479 The complete table 'Expected Cross Tabulation: Perception of Social Advertising and Informational Social Web Usage' can be found in the appendix.

age and the perception of social advertising ($p > 0.05$). The following diagram presents the different means:[480]

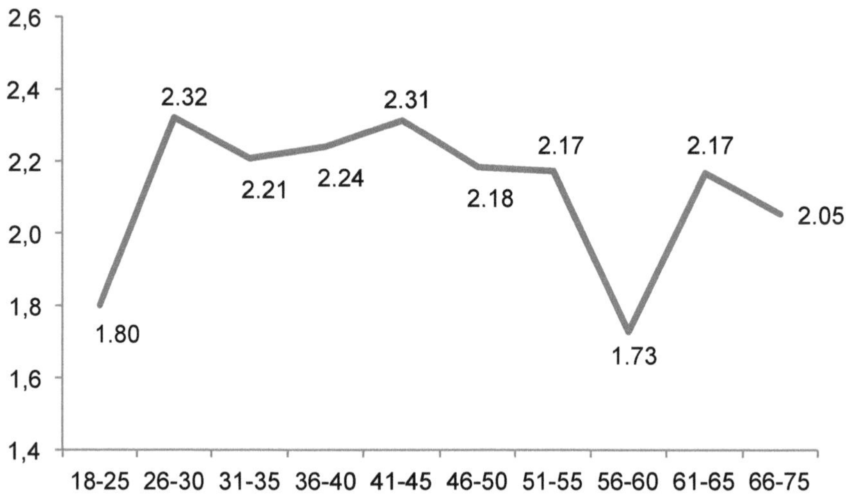

Fig. 44: Means: Attitude towards Social Advertising Perception by Age. Source: own survey

As can be clearly seen, there is no general trend regarding the perception of social advertising. Users aged 18 to 25 and 56 to 60 show a more positive than average attitude while users aged 26 to 30 and 41 to 45 perceive social advertising more negatively than the average. According to the t-test,[481] this difference is significant ($p < 0.05$). The ANOVA also states a significant effect of the age on the perception of social advertising ($p < 0.05$).[482] According to the univariate ANCOVA, no significance arises ($p > 0.05$). The correlation analysis presents a correlation coefficient towards zero ($p > 0.05$) and hence reveals that there is no linear correlation between both variables.

The general social web usage and the specific social information search could be identified as the only factors influencing the perception of social advertising.

480 The means may range from 1 to 3 (1 = positive view, 2 = neutral view, 3 = negative view). The data were recoded.

481 For the independent t-test younger users were defined by the age 18 to 55 while older users were defined by the age 56 to 75.

482 The ANOVA has been carried out separately for the different social web sites.

When considering all participants, the general acceptance of social advertising is rather neutral.

6.3.5.2 Discussion of Research Hypothesis V

As social advertising is becoming more and more popular for hotels, RH V examined how users perceive this form of advertising.

In total, 28.1% of all the considered participants have already clicked on an online ad banner on the social web, which indicates that social advertising is appreciated by a rather small subset. Whereas 36% have a negative attitude towards social advertising, only 19% have a positive attitude. 45% have an indifferent view.

Regarding the question if there are certain user characteristics that induce a positive or negative attitude towards social advertising, RH V presented distinct differences. There is a correlation between the general social web usage and the perception of social ads. Frequent social web users have a more positive to neutral attitude than occasional users, most probably because they are more accustomed to social advertising. This relation is even more intense when considering the degree of how the social web is used as a source of information. Users who gather information on the social web perceive social ads distinctly more positive than those who do not use the social web as an information source. This distinctness is especially strong for users who gather information on social networks and on media sharing platforms. The informational use of hotel review sites and travel communities is also significantly related to the perception of social advertising. The significance of these results for hotels is immediately recognizable: the corporate objective, when placing social advertisements online, is to attract the users' attention on a platform where they spend their freetime. With social advertising, hotels may lead users to the hotel's own social web sites with the superior aim to increase brand awareness and sales. Users who are looking for hotel information on the social web mostly do so because they want to book a hotel room. As these users partially have a positive view on social advertising, hotels may 'catch' them with their ad banners during their information search, a process that may even lead to a direct booking. From this point of view, placing advertisements on the social web can be supported and approved.

Furthermore, analyses regarding travel frequency as well as demographic characteristics were also conducted. It was elaborated that the perception of social advertising does not differ between frequent and occasional travellers. Gender does not have an impact on the attitude towards social advertising either. A general trend regarding the age could not be detected either. These findings imply that no limitations regarding the target group of social advertising exist, but that guests may be attracted by social advertising independently from their travel frequency and demographic characteristics.

It has to be acknowledged that only about one quarter of the sample group reported having already clicked on a social ad banner and that the general acceptance of social advertising is rather neutral. The placing of social ads therefore shows severe limitations and should be carefully considered.

6.4 Cluster Analysis

Finally, the question arises if among social web users different information behavioural types can be defined. This issue is analyzed with the help of a cluster analysis. The two-step cluster analysis has been applied, as it is recommended when analyzing a large quantity of data.[483] The aim of the analysis is to differentiate the hotel guests who use the social web as an information source. The conducted two-step cluster analysis presents two clusters.[484] The users of cluster 1 are referred to as *advanced social information seekers* while cluster 2 consists of *basic social information seekers*. The following table gives an overview of the characteristics:

	advanced social information seekers (44.1%)	**basic social information seekers** (55.9%)
reporting on hotel review sites (1 = frequently, 2 = occasionally, 3 = never, 4 = never heard of it)	1.92	2.78
retrieving information on hotel review sites (1 = a lot, 2 = a little, 3 = not at all, 4 = never heard of it)	1.37	2.27
general usage of booking sites with review function (1 = daily, 2 = several times a week, 3 = weekly, 4 = less often, 5 = never heard of it)	3.25	4.13

483 Cf. Brosius 2011, p. 761

484 The following variables were considered for the cluster analysis: general social web usage, integration of the social web sites into the information process, degree of personal reporting, degree of impact of the social web's content on the personal booking decision as well as the attitude towards social bookings. Other variables were also considered at first, however, turned out to be not decisive.

	advanced social information seekers (44.1%)	basic social information seekers (55.9%)
reporting on booking sites with review function (1 = frequently, 2 = occasionally, 3 = never, 4 = never heard of it)	2.08	2.8
general usage of hotel review sites (1 = daily, 2 = several times a week, 3 = weekly, 4 = less often, 5 = never heard of it)	3.31	4.11
general usage of travel communities (1 = daily, 2 = several times a week, 3 = weekly, 4 = less often, 5 = never heard of it)	3.89	4.82
retrieving information on booking sites with review function (1 = a lot, 2 = a little, 3 = not at all, 4 = never heard of it)	1.57	2.27
impact of hotel review sites (1 = high, 2 = some, 3 = few, 4 = never heard of it)	1.24	1.87
retrieving information on travel communities (1 = a lot, 2 = a little, 3 = not at all, 4 = never heard of it)	2.41	2.97
social bookings acceptance (1 = yes, 2 = no)	1.54	1.9
retrieving information on social networks (1 = a lot, 2 = a little, 3 = not at all, 4 = never heard of it)	2.62	2.99
impact of booking sites with review function (1 =high, 2 = some, 3 = few, 4 = never heard of it)	1.45	1.98
general social web usage (1 = daily, 2 = several times a week, 3 = weekly, 4 = less often, 5 = never heard of it)	2.62	3.19
general usage of social networks (1 = daily, 2 = several times a week, 3 = weekly, 4 = less often, 5 = never heard of it)	3.07	3.78

Table 34: Cluster Analysis. Order of the variables by importance of the predictive factors. Source: own survey

Advanced social information seekers are regular social web users who access the social web at least once a week. They visit social networks, hotel review sites and booking sites with review function weekly and travel communities less than weekly. The social web plays an integrated part during their information search. Hotel review sites are frequented a lot and booking sites with review function a lot to a little. The degree of the information process exceeds the basic social information search and partly also includes the information gathering on travel communities and social networks. Advanced information seekers are highly influenced by reviews. They are not only passive consumers but also prosumers who actively publish reviews themselves. They have a neutral opinion on social bookings.

Basic social information seekers, in contrast, access the social web weekly. They use hotel review sites, booking sites with review function and social networks less than weekly and mostly do not use travel communities at all. During their hotel information gathering, they consider the most popular social web sites, namely hotel review sites and booking sites with review function a little while other sites are neglected. Basic social information seekers do not take reviews too seriously but acknowledge only some impact on the personal booking decision. They are pure information consumers and do not share experiences themselves. The possibility of social bookings is not appreciated.

The differences between both clusters can also be summarized graphically:[485]

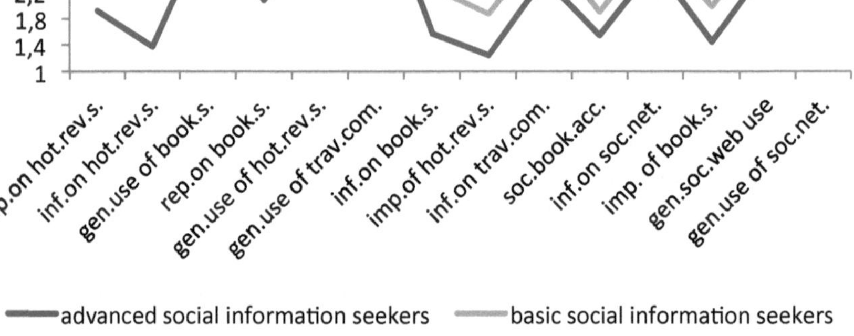

Fig. 45: Cluster Analysis: Advanced and Basic Social Information Seekers. Source: own survey

485 For reasons of clarity the different means are not displayed.

As can be seen, the means of advanced social information seekers are exceptionless lower than the means of basic social information seekers. Hence, advanced social information seekers use the social web more intensively and in a more sophisticated way during their information search.

The cluster analysis shows that there are two types of guests who are using the social web as a source of information: *advanced* social information seekers consider not only the classic social web applications but also sites like travel communities and social networks. Additionally, they also contribute content themselves. *Basic* social information seekers use popular social web sites for the information gathering to a far lesser extent. While the basic information seekers do not share their experiences on the social web, reviews of advanced social information seekers may have a significant impact on the decision of others. Looking back on chapter 2, where Kotler's five-phase model and the filtering effect of the social web were depicted, the post sale evaluation of advanced social information seekers may be seen as an influencing factor for the information process of other social web users. The distribution of both clusters is similar, with 44.1% advanced and 55.9% basic social information seekers.

The two clusters are also analyzed by their travel and demographic characteristics. Both clusters consist almost equally of men and women and regarding age no distinct difference can be detected. Cluster 1 shows a higher travel frequency, with 57.5% of users having five and more hotel stays per year. In cluster 2, only 44% of users have five and more hotel stays per year. Hence, advanced social information seekers have a higher travel frequency than basic social information seekers. The fact that the travel frequency is the only differentiating characteristic between both clusters supports the findings of the previous research hypotheses, according to which travel and demographic characteristics were mostly not decisive for the degree of informational social web usage either.

The cluster analysis shows that users who access the social web as a source of information can be divided into two groups. Whereas basic social information seekers are not very interesting from a hotel's perspective, as they consider only popular social web sites and do not contribute own content, the future lies on advanced social information seekers. As they also integrate travel communities and social networks and fill the social web with content, they will boost the social web's further development and expansion. The fact that they make up almost 50% of all social information seekers is evaluated very positively.

7 Concluding Remarks

7.1 Summary of the Research Hypotheses

The focus of this paper was to determine to what extent the social web influences the information search of hotel guests. In order to do so, five research hypotheses were defined. Their findings are briefly summarized in the following paragraphs.

RH I: The informational social web usage depends on travel frequency and the general social web usage.

RH I was formulated in order to test if the informational use of the social web depends on particular user characteristics regarding travel frequency and general social web usage.

RH I identified hotel review sites and booking sites with review function as the most important source of information. Social networks, travel communities and media sharing platforms are also considered during the information process, however, are less intensively used. Blogs & podcasts and microblogs were identified as insignificant sites for the information search.

Regarding travel frequency, it was elaborated that the social web is mainly used by both frequent and occasional travellers. The general social web usage is decisive for the degree of informational social web usage. The majority of social web applications is accessed more often as an information source with increasing general social web usage.

RH II: The informational social web usage differs between the younger generation and best agers.

As best agers generally use the social web less frequently than younger users – although one has witnessed high growth rates within the last years, according to chapter 2 – the question arose as to whether they can be reached at all on the social web.

The analyses of RH II could not determine distinct differences in the informational usage between the age groups. In fact, best agers sometimes even exceeded the younger generation, e.g. when reporting about their hotel experiences on the social web. Concluding from the statistical analyses, best agers can be as equally reached as younger users. However, one has to bear in mind that the total number of best agers, using the social web is by far smaller than the number of younger users and hence predominantly younger users can be reached on the social web.

RH III: The varying social web sites have a different impact on the personal hotel booking decision.

The aim of RH III was to define the impact of the social web's different sites. Additionally, it examined whether the impact on users can be generalized or if some users can be more easily influenced than others.

The general impact of negative reviews on the personal booking decision could be attested with almost 30% of the considered participants stating to have already withdrawn their existing booking decision due to negative reviews.

The biggest impact on the personal hotel booking decision could be acknowledged for reviews on hotel review sites and booking sites with review function. In addition, reviews and comments on social networks, travel communities and media sharing platforms were also identified as influencing factors, although their impact is lower.

It already became apparent that no distinct differences regarding informational social web usage and travel frequency as well as demographic characteristics occur. This could also be proven in RH III, where only a negligible impact could be determined for both travel frequency and demographic characteristics. The only influencing variable ist the general social web usage: the impact increases with growing usage.

RH IV: The social web has the potential to evolve into a relevant distribution channel.

As presented in chapter 2, the social web offers the possibility to make social bookings. With this in mind, it was to investigate whether social bookings have the potential to develop into a relevant distribution channel. Generally, 27% of the considered participants stated that they would book their hotel room directly on the social web. With 73% claiming no positive affinity to social bookings, a certain reluctance to this new distribution possibility becomes apparent. However, bearing the background of increasing social web usage and growing importance of online bookings, it is likely that the attitude towards social bookings will become more positive in the future.

The current acceptance of social bookings is higher for users who already gather information on the social web. These users mostly search for information because they have to book a hotel room. Hence, they present an important target group to hotels, as hotels may approach these users during their information search and lead them to their social bookings possibility. Since the analyses presented a special significance for social networks, a booking widget on the hotel's Facebook fan page seems to be recommendable. Again, the analysis of travel frequency and demographic characteristics did not reveal great differences.

RH V: The perception of social advertising depends on particular user characteristics.

As placing advertisements on the social web is becoming more popular for hotels, RH V was defined in order to judge the users' perception of social advertising. From all the considered participants, 28% have already clicked on an ad banner on the social web. This rather small number indicates that social advertising is currently appreciated only by a small share of guests. However, the perception of social advertising becomes more positive with increasing general social web usage and specifically with increasing informational social web usage. As users who are looking for information about hotels mostly also have to book a hotel room later on, they may be attracted by social ad banners. As the calculations were especially significant for social networks and media sharing platforms, placing advertisements on these sites in particular seems to be beneficial. Again, the analysis of travel frequency and demographic characteristics did not show significant differences.

7.2 Implications of the Findings

Currently, there seems to be a great hype about the social web. The number of its users are continuously increasing and in addition to that, corporate participation is growing. The social web appears to be especially applicable to high-involvement hotel services, which are generally characterized by a great need for information. UGC seems to provide a valuable way for hotel guests to gather information. Hotels, on the other hand, have vast possibilities to present their services and to authentically interact with their guests. From this point of view, it is easy to assume that the social web plays a very important part in hotel industry for both guests and hotels. However, the findings of this paper suggest a different conclusion. Although a certain degree of importance is definitely acknowledged, the social web's impact is not as strong as it is generally presumed.

As tourist information gathering is a subconscious process that cannot be measured precisely, the exact impact of the social web is difficult to define. Nevertheless, the paper provides suggestions of how the social web is being considered during the information process. The following paragraphs will present its impacts on guests and hotels.

7.2.1 Impact of the Social Web on Hotel Guests

The social web has induced vast changes, regarding possibilities for the information search.[486] As the most reliable information is collected through personal communication and the private exchange of experiences,[487] the UGC presents perfect opportunities for information gathering. Additionally, the social web may even stimulate the need for a hotel overnight stay in the first place, as shown in chapter 3 by presenting the extension of Kotler's five-phase model. Theoretically, the social web could cause enormous changes to information processes.

However, the importance of the social web has severe limitations. The social web is mostly used as a source of information by frequent social web users. This survey included a great number of participants who stated that they do not use the social web at all. Hence, it is useful to only a subset of guests.

The general usage of the social web is decisive for the degree of how the social web is used as a source of information. The sample group was analyzed according to their different travel frequency and demographic characteristics. Between frequent and occasional travellers, men and women and younger and older users, mostly no distinct differences in informational usage arose. In fact, a trend to homogeneity could be detected. This trend to homogeneity, which is most certainly also correlated with the methodological approach of the survey, presents an important finding. It shows that the social web has surpassed its introduction phase: in the beginning, innovations are mostly considered only by a small number of pioneers. With further development, innovations diffuse and are used by different groups of people. The social web has exceeded its innovation status and has expanded in multiple directions. This can be supported by the fact that the social web is also used by best agers. If the same study had been conducted five years ago, most probably only younger people would have stated that they use the social web. They were born as digital natives and are accustomed to the digital world and its innovations.[488] However, today, also best agers appreciate the social web and its possibilities. Although the total number of best agers using the social web is by far smaller than the number of the younger users, best agers who use the social web in general also actively access it during the information process. As best agers were

486 Cf. Xiang 2011, p. 343, in: Law et al. 2011

487 Cf. Wöhler 1993, p. 157, in: Hahn et al. 1993

488 Cf. Prensky 2001, p.1

not born as digital natives and are hence not generally as advanced in Internet usage as the younger generation, the active usage of them is especially significant. The social web's use has spread to different groups. This diffusion took place quietly and without much public awareness. The social web is still considered to be a 'niche' product. However, the findings of this paper regarding characteristics of informational social web users proves a different perception. It shows that the social web's acceptance is established and that it is accessed mostly independently from demographic characteristics. This was also supported by the cluster analysis, in which the different clusters, namely advanced and basic social information seekers, could not be characterized by any demographic attributes.

Currently, the informational focus is on hotel review sites and booking sites with review function, which are accessed the most as a source of information. However, travel communities, social networks and media sharing platforms provide valuable information to guests as well. Apparently, blogs & podcasts and microblogs seem to be of no interest, as they are neglected during the information gathering process.

A decisive distinction between the informational social web users is the degree of active participation in the social web. The study showed that the majority of users is passive consumers who only collect information but do not share reviews themselves. The great majority of active users share reviews on hotel review sites and booking sites with review function. Only a small – but very important – subset also actively contribute content on other social web sites.

Currently, users who integrate the social web into their information process can be divided into two types: basic and advanced social information seekers. Basic social information seekers orientate themselves mainly towards the popular social web applications hotel review sites and booking sites with review function. As shown in chapter 2 they are spectators and do not actively contribute content. They would not book their hotel room on the social web and acknowledge only little influence of reviews on their own booking decision. The more interesting target group for hotels is advanced social information seekers, as they may indicate where development is heading. Advanced social information seekers go beyond the classic social web sites and also consider travel communities and social networks. As they are contributors and share their own experiences and reviews, they affect the booking decision of others significantly. In addition, they fuel the social web's further development. As with each day, the social web is becoming an increasingly important part of the daily life and as people are getting more accustomed to using it, there is a great future potential for an increase in advanced social information seekers.

7.2.2 Impact of the Social Web on Hotels

The social web offers vast possibilities for hotels to engage with their guests. Especially against the background of the fact that the German hotel market is predominantly characterized by small businesses,[489] which mostly have small budget for marketing activities, as well as the fact that there are currently great overcapacities,[490] the social web provides efficient possibilities for hotels to engage with their customers. Additionally, the communication on the social web is not limited to German guests but can reach guests worldwide. Especially with regard to the fact that foreign guests generated more than 60 million overnight stays in 2010,[491] this opens huge opportunities. As depicted in detail in chapter 2, the participation in the social web has evolved into a popular marketing strategy. Hotels seem to engage with enthusiasm, often operating a Facebook fan page or a Twitter channel of their own. However, this enthusiasm has to be considered carefully against the background of the paper's findings.

The study showed that the social web is used as a source of information. However, the usage shows certain limitations. Currently, guests focus very much on the popular social web applications namely hotel review sites and booking sites with review function. There is only a rather small subset that can be reached via social networks, travel communities and media sharing platforms. However, if the recent development in social web usage continues, the number of guests approaching these channels should increase. Therefore, social networks, travel communities and media sharing platforms may further gain in importance. Blogs & podcasts and microblogs were identified as inconsequential social web applications for information gathering; their climax in significance has passed. They may be important sites for other tourist services, however, they are perceived as minor regarding the gathering of information about hotels. The insignificance of blogs and microblogs was also confirmed by another study in 2012, where European city travellers were questioned about their information gathering.[492] Hence, a hotel participation in blogs & podcasts and microblogs is not recommended at this point. However, as it is observed and also supported by corporate social web studies, presented in chapter 2, Twitter seems to be a popular way of communication for hotels. In the setting of the findings of RH I, this participation should be strongly reconsidered.

489 Cf. IHA 2011, p. 34

490 Cf. IHA 2011, p. 34

491 Cf. IHA 2011, p. 58

492 Cf. Raab 2012, p. 150f.

The study proved that reviews on social web sites significantly impact the personal booking decision. The impact of reviews on hotel review sites and booking sites with review function is especially high. However, reviews and comments on social networks, travel communities and media sharing platforms may also influence the booking decision of others significantly. It therefore becomes obvious once more that negative reviews have to be avoided by all means.

Generally, there is a strong affinity for online bookings of hotel accommodations.[493] However, the survey showed that the current acceptance of social bookings is rather reluctant. Only about one quarter of the considered participants would book their hotel room on social web sites. The probability of conducting social bookings is higher for users who are already looking for information on the social web. As these users mostly also have to book a hotel room, hotels may attract them during their online information process and may lead them to the hotel's social bookings facility. The analyses were especially significant for social networks. Against the background of chapter 4, presenting that the direct online booking is connected with the fewest charges, the corporate advantages of social bookings are assessed positively. However, the current users' opinion is rather reserved.

Regarding social advertising, a certain degree of reluctance becomes apparent. In total, about 27% of all the considered participants have already clicked on ad banners on the social web. Only 19% have a positive while 36% have a negative attitude towards social advertising. 45% reported an indifference. However, when considering especially those guests who are looking for information on the social web, the perception becomes more positive. Therefore, hotels can use social advertising to attract guests who are using the social web as a source of information. Since these guests probably also need to book a hotel room, they may present an interesting target group.

The study investigated travel frequency and demographic characteristics of social web users. Mostly, no distinct differences could be found. Frequent and occasional travellers both access the social web as a source of information. Also, best agers may be addressed by hotels on the social web, as they proved to search for information on social web sites as well. Since they generally present an interesting target group for hotels, the communication with them on social web sites provides valuable opportunities.

The fact that older guests also use the social web as an information source – commonly assumed rather not to use it – shows that the prevailing marketing

493 Cf. VIR 2012, p. 21

assumptions have to be reassessed. As the social web has diffused into different directions and is used by guests with various characteristics, a precise definition of guests using the social web cannot be given.

The social web is not a universal marketing strategy and guests who only consider the traditional marketing media cannot be reached on the social web. This entails that the social web approaches only a subset of the guest mix and will not substitute traditional marketing activities. Nevertheless, a corporate participation is recommended. The social web provides valuable possibilities to authentically engage with guests and to promote communication. Even if the number of guests using these opportunities is comparably low, there are guests who can be reached on the social web and who should not be neglected.

There is also another reason to participate in the social web: since 2011, tourist information gathering and decision making has been made along the so-called social graph.[494] The social graph consists of the entity of the user's relations and contacts.[495] In order to positively influence the guests in their booking decision, hotels should try to become part of the guests' social graphs by engaging with them on the social web. Also, as explained in chapter 3, the social web may generate the need for a hotel accommodation in the first place. With their active participation in the social web, hotels may initiate the need themselves and attract new and existing customers.

However, the participation has to be carefully considered and should always be seen as an additional and not as a stand-alone strategy. As studies showed, many companies become active without having a strategy[496] or monitoring the activities. This should be avoided by all means. The participation in the social web has to be taken care of conscientiously.

The participation in the social web should be seen as a medium to long-term investment. As studies have shown, the most mentioned reasons for the corporate social web presence are the increase in brand popularity and customer loyalty, as well as the acquisition of new customers.[497] While the last factor may be measureable – although it is often hard to define where and how exactly the new guest was acquired – brand popularity and customer loyalty are difficult to measure. Hence, the success of the activities is difficult to assess.

494 Cf. Amersdorffer et al. 2010, p. 8f., in: Amersdorffer et al. 2010

495 Cf. Amersdorffer et al. 2010, p. 386, in: Amersdorffer et al. 2010

496 View chapter 2.6

497 Cf. eCircle 2011, p. 9f.

7.3 Outlook and Further Thoughts

The paper proved a general importance of the social web for the hotel industry. Currently, it is rather a small subset which integrates the social web's content into the information search. However, considering the development of the social web's usage of recent years, it is most likely to witness further growth in the future. Presumably, the *informational* use of the social web is only at its beginnings. Social web sites, which are currently accessed mostly by advanced information seekers, may gain in importance and will most likely also be accessed by basic information seekers in the future. Hence, basic information seekers may slowly progress into advanced social information seekers. However, this process will take some further time to develop.

The paper gave an overview of the social web's current status quo and indicated in which direction the development is heading. As the social web is embedded into a dynamic and quickly changing environment, its future progress is difficult to predict. Chapter 2 presented that location-based services will further develop, presenting interesting future possibilities, especially for last-minute hotel bookings in the surrounding area. As presented in chapter 2, according to Amersdorffer et al.,[498] the social web will become an individual travel companion. With regard to the increasing use of the mobile web, this also entails that guests are able to share their experiences not only after their departure but also during their stay, which in turn offers numerous new possibilities for corporate communication.

The evaluation of the quality of communication is seen as an interesting aspect. Future studies may further asses the degree of dialogue in the communication between guests and hotels. As this paper presents only a snapshot of the current state of affairs and due to the fact that there are extensive and continuous changes regarding the Internet and especially regarding the social web, follow-up studies in a few years might be promising.

Although there seem to be endless future possibilities, it once again needs to be stated that the social web will not substitute the traditional marketing: there will always remain guests who simply do not use the Internet – let alone the social web – and can only be approached via traditional marketing activities. Therefore, companies should continue incorporating traditional marketing activities also in the future.

The paper presents only findings for the hotel information process and may therefore not be applicable to other tourist services. If the same study had been

498 Cf. Amersdorffer et al. 2010, p. 8f., in: Amersdorffer et al. 2010

conducted in a different environment, e.g. the hostel industry, the results would have possibly differed. Additionally, the study investigated the information process of German hotel guests. As shown in chapter 2, US users prove to apply a more advanced social web usage. Therefore a study questioning US hotel guests may reveal different results.

Bibliography

Absatzwirtschaft.de (editor) (a): Warum auch schlechte Bewertungen gut fürs Geschäft sein können, n.n. 2012, http://www.absatzwirtschaft.de/content/online-marketing/news/warum-auch-schlechte-bewertungen-gut-fuers-geschaeft-sein-koennen;77634, accessed on 09.09.2012

Absatzwirtschaft.de (editor) (b): Wie Marketingstrategien im Shitstorm enden und was zu tun ist, n.n. 2012, http://www.absatzwirtschaft.de/content/online-marketing/news/wie-marketingstrategien-im-shitstorm-enden-und-was-zu-tun-ist;77939, accessed on 15.09.2012

Absatzwirtschaft.de (editor): Reisebranche plant Investitionen in Mobile Commerce, n.n. 2011, http://www.absatzwirtschaft.de/content/marketingstrategie/news/reisebranche-plant-investitionen-in-mobile-commerce;74099, accessed on 15.10.2011

ADAC Verlag (editor): Reise-Monitor 2011. Trendforschung im Reisemarkt 1995-2011, n.n. 2011, http://media.adac.de/mediaservice/studien.html, accessed on 20.11.2011

AGOF (editor): Ergebnisse mobile facts 2012-I – pdf, n.n. 2012, http://www.agof.de/aktuelle-studie.1022.de.html, accessed on 01.10.2012

allfacebook.de (editor): Buchungswidget auf Facebook verwenden, n.n. 2010, http://allfacebook.de/beyond/buchungswidget-auf-facebook-verwenden-tourismus-themenspecial/, accessed on 15.09.2011

Alpar, Paul; Blaschke, Steffen; Keßler, Steffen: Web 2.0. Neue erfolgreiche Kommunikationsstrategien für kleine und mittlere Unternehmen. Hessisches Ministerium für Wirtschaft, Verkehr und Landesentwicklung, Hessen Media Band 57, Wiesbaden 2007

Alterian.de (editor): Sieben Gründe für Corporate Social Media Monitoring, n.n. 2010, http://www.alterian.de/ressourcen/ArtikelWhitepapers/Sieben_Grunde_fur_Corporate_Social_Media_Monitoring.pdf/, accessed on 07.07.2012

Amersdorffer, Daniel; Bauhuber, Florian; Egger, Roman; Oellrich, Jens (editors): Social Web im Tourismus. Strategien – Konzepte – Einsatzfelder, Berlin 2010

Amersdorffer, Daniel; *Bauhuber, Florian; Oellrich, Jens*: Das Social Web – Internet, Gesellschaft, Tourismus, Zukunft, in: Amersdorffer et al. 2010, p. 3-16

Anderson, Chris: The Long Tail. Nischenprodukte statt Massenmarkt, München 2008

ARD/ZDF (editor) (a): ARD/ZDF-Onlinestudie 2012: Entwicklung Onlinenutzung, n.n. 2012,
http://www.ard-zdf-onlinestudie.de/index.php?id=onlinenutzung000, accessed on 01.09.2012

ARD/ZDF (editor) (b): ARD/ZDF-Onlinestudie 2012: Internetnutzer in Mio., n.n. 2012,
http://www.ard-zdf-onlinestudie.de/index.php?id=onlinenutzung-mio0, accessed on 01.09.2012

ARD/ZDF (editor) (c): ARD/ZDF-Onlinestudie 2012: Verweildauer, n.n. 2012,
http://www.ard-zdf-onlinestudie.de/index.php?id=366, accessed on 01.09.2012

ARD/ZDF (editor) (d): ARD/ZDF-Onlinestudie 2012: Internetzugang, n.n. 2012,
http://www.ard-zdf-onlinestudie.de/index.php?id=361, accessed on 01.09.2012

ARD/ZDF (editor) (e): ARD/ZDF-Onlinestudie 2012: Nutzung, n.n. 2012,
http://www.ard-zdf-onlinestudie.de/index.php?id=357, accessed on 01.09.2012

ARD/ZDF (editor) (f): ARD/ZDF-Onlinestudie 2012: Mobile Nutzung, n.n. 2012,
http://www.ard-zdf-onlinestudie.de/index.php?id=362, accessed on 01.09.2012

ARD/ZDF (editor) (g): ARD/ZDF-Onlinestudie 2012: Nutzung, n.n. 2012,
http://www.ard-zdf-onlinestudie.de/index.php?id=354, accessed on 01.09.2012

ARD/ZDF (editor) (h): ARD/ZDF-Onlinestudie 2012: Genutzte Anwendungen, n.n. 2012, http://www.ard-zdf-onlinestudie.de/index.php?id=onlinenutzunganwend0, accessed on 01.09.2012

Back, Andrea (editor): Web 2.0 in der Unternehmenspraxis: Grundlagen, Fallstudien und Trends zum Einsatz von Social Software, München 2009

Bänsch, Axel: Käuferverhalten, München 2002

Bastian, Harald (editor): Tourismus 3.0. Fakten und Perspektiven, Hamburg 2009

Bastian, Harald; Kauley, Anne; Wilmsmeyer, Daniela: Web 2.0 und Social Software. Status Quo und Chancen für die Touristik, in: Bastian 2009, n.n.

Becker, Christoph; Hopfinger, Hans; Steinecke, Albrecht: Geographie der Freizeit und des Tourismus, München 2003

Bernauer, Dominik; Hesse, Gero; Laick, Steffen; Schmitz, Bernd: Social Media im Personalmarketing, Köln 2011

Bitkom.org (editor): 'Connected Worlds'. Wie Lebens- und Technikwelten zusammen wachsen, n.n. 2010, http://www.bitkom.org/files/documents/BITKOM_Connected_Worlds_Extranet.pdf, accessed on 28.09.2012

Boksberger, Philipp; Schnuckert, Markus (editors): Innovationen in Tourismus und Freizeit, Berlin 2011

Bosold, Joachim: Gästebefragung, in: Hahn et al. 1993, p. 539-541

Brosius, Felix: SPSS 19, München 2011

Buss, Anna: Internet Marketing: Erfolgreich planen, gestalten, umsetzen, München 2009

BVDW: Social Media Kompass 2010/2011, Düsseldorf 2010

Cornell University (editor): How Travelers use Online and Social Media Channels to Make Hotel-choice Decisions, n.n. 2010, http://www.hotelschool.cornell.edu/research/chr/pubs/reports/abstract-15359.html, accessed on 15.09.2012

De Ascaniis, Silvia; Morasso, Sara Greco: When tourists give their reasons on the web: the argumentative significance of tourism related UGC, in: Law et al. 2011, p. 125-136

DEHOGA: Definition der Betriebsarten, n.n. 2011, http://www.dehoga-bundesverband.de/daten-fakten-trends/betriebsarten/, accessed on 05.05.2011

DEHOGA: DEHOGA Konjunkturumfrage Sommer 2010 – Ausblick Winter 2010/2011, n.n. 2010, http://www.dehoga-bundesverband.de/fileadmin/Inhaltsbilder/Daten_Fakten_Trends/Zahlespiegel_und_Branchenberichte/Branchenbericht/DEHOGA-Branchenbericht_Sommer_2010.pdf, accessed on 10.05.2011

DIVSI (editor): DIVSI Milieu Studie zu Vertrauen und Sicherheit im Internet, n.n. 2012, https://www.divsi.de/divsi-milieu-studie, accessed on 10.09.2012

Ebersbach, Anja; Glaser, Markus; Heigl, Richard: Social Web, Konstanz 2008

Ebersbach, Anja; Glaser, Markus; Heigl, Richard: Social Web, 2nd edition, Konstanz 2010

eCircle (editor): Der Europäische Social Media und E-Mail Monitor – 6 Länder Studie zum digitalen Dialog mit Facebook, Twitter, E-Mail & Co. (Ergebnisse Deutschland Teil 3 – Entscheider-Befragung), n.n. 2011, http://www.ecircle.com/fileadmin/files/pdfs/04_Resource_Centre/4.4._Studien/DE/Social_Media_E-Mail_Studie_2011-_Expertenbefragung.pdf, accessed on 15.07.2012

eCircle (editor): Der Europäische Social Media und E-Mail Monitor – 6 Länder Studie zum digitalen Dialog mit Facebook, Twitter, E-Mail & Co. (Ergebnisse Deutschland Teil 1), n.n. 2010, http://de.slideshare.net/SocialMediaCuts/e-circle-der-europische-social-media-und-email-monitor1010, accessed on 15.07.2012

Egger, Roman; Jooss, Mario; Schmeisser, Sabine: Informationsverhalten von Freizeitreisenden im Kontext kultureller Besonderheiten, in: Lassnig et al. 2010, p. 19-28

Eisenstein, Bernd; Rosinski, André: Economic Effects of the Tourism, in: Becker et al. 2003, p. 805-814

Elcario.de (editor): Twitter on Paper – Zahlen, Daten und Fakten im April 2010, n.n. 2010, http://www.elcario.de/twitter-on-paper-zahlen-daten-und-fakten-im-april-2010/849/, accessed on 09.06.2011

Faber, Michael (editor) (a): TOUROM-Studie 2011 – Highlights, n.n. 2011, http://www.touristikconsulting.de/download/TOUROM_Studie_2011_Highlights.pdf, accessed on 05.08.2012

Faber, Michael (editor) (b): Social Media in der Hotellerie. Voruntersuchung zur TOUROM Studie 2011: Social Media in der Reisebranche, n.n. 2011, http://de.slideshare.net/mifaber/social-media-in-der-hotellerie#btnNext, accessed on 10.08.2012

Fabian, Romy: Kundenkommunikation über Social Media, Köln 2011

Facebook (editor): ITS Urlaubsdeals, n.n. 2012, https://www.facebook.com/its-reisen?sk=app_418450704858321, accessed on 25.09.2012

Facebook-werbung.com (editor): Facebook-Werbung. Streuverlust war gestern. Facebook ist heute., n.n. 2010-2012, http://www.facebook-werbung.com/was-kostets/, accessed on 19.10.2012

FAZ.net (editor) (a): 20 Millionen Nutzer in Deutschland, n.n. 2011, http://www.faz.net/aktuell/wirtschaft/netzwirtschaft/der-facebook-boersengang/facebook-20-millionen-nutzer-in-deutschland-1635751.html, accessed on 15.09.2012

FAZ.net (editor) (b): Folgt auf den E-Commerce der Facebook-Commerce?, n.n. 2011, http://faz-community.faz.net/blogs/netzwirtschaft-blog/archive/2011/06/09/folgt-auf-den-e-commerce-der-f-commerce.aspx, accessed on 17.06.2011

Feil, Thomas; Oertel, Britta; Sie Liong, Thio: E-Business im öffentlichen Tourismussektor: Nutzung und Anwendung von Informations- und Kommunikationstechnologien im europäischen Vergleich, in: Becker et al. 2003, p. 428-440

Fesenmaier, Daniel R.; Xiang, Zheng; Pan, Bing; Law, Rob: An Analysis of Search Engine Use for Travel Planning, in: Gretzel et al. 2010, p. 381-392

Fink & Fuchs (editor): Social Media Governance 2010, n.n. 2010, http://www.ffpr.de/newsroom/2010/08/25/social-media-governance-2010/, accessed on 15.09.2011

Focus online (editor): Facebook nutzt E-Mail-Adresse für Werbung, n.n. 2012, http://www.focus.de/digital/internet/netzoekonomie-blog/nutzung-mail-adressen-und-telefonnummern-facebook-ermoeglicht-unternehmen-zielgerichtete-werbung_aid_810287.html, accessed on 14.09.2012

Focus online (editor): Google+ lässt ab heute jeden rein, n.n. 2011, http://www.focus.de/digital/internet/google/facebook-konkurrenz-google-laesst-ab-heute-jeden-rein_aid_667460.html, accessed on 01.05.2012

Forrester Research (editor): Forrester's new Social Technographic Report, n.n. 2007, http://forrester.typepad.com/groundswell/2007/04/forresters_new_.html, accessed on 01.09.2011

FredCavazza.net: Social Media Landscape, n.n., http://www.fredcavazza.net/2008/06/09/social-media-landscape/, accessed on 01.10.2012

Freyer, Walter: Tourismus. Eine Einführung in die Fremdenverkehrsökonomie, 8th edition, München 2006

FTD.de (editor): Unternehmen hören Usern zu wenig zu, n.n. 2011, http://www.ftd.de/karriere/management/:social-media-nutzung-unternehmen-hoeren-usern-zu-wenig-zu/60049734.html, accessed on 10.09.2012

Futurebiz (editor) (a): Content in sozialen Netzwerken: US-Nutzer produzieren und Deutsche konsumieren, n.n. 2012, http://www.futurebiz.de/artikel/content-in-sozialen-netzwerken-us-nutzer-produzieren-und-deutsche-konsumieren/, accessed on 06.09.2012

Futurebiz (editor) (b): Übersicht Social Media Tools – Content-Management, Monitoring & sozialen Features [Infografik], n.n. 2012, http://www.futurebiz.de/artikel/ubersicht-social-media-tools-content-management-monitoring-sozialen-features-infografik/, accessed on 10.09.2012

Futurebiz (editor): Facebook Nutzerzahlen: Nutzer werden immer älter, n.n. 2010, http://www.futurebiz.de/artikel/facebook-nutzerzahlen-nutzer-werden-immer-alter/, accessed on 01.07.2011

Gardini, Marco A.: Marketing-Management in der Hotellerie, München 2003

Gehrke, Gernot (editor): Web 2.0 – Schlagwort oder Megatrend, Marl 2007

Gehrke, Gernot; Gräßer, Lars: Neues Web, neue Kompetenz, in: Gehrke 2007, p. 11-36

Google Trends (editor): TripAdvisor, n.n. 2012, http://www.google.com/trends/?q=TripAdvisor&ctab=0&geo=all&date=all&sort=0, accessed on 14.09.2012

Gräf, Lorenz: Online-Befragung. Eine praktische Einführung für Anfänger, Berlin 2010

Gretzel, Ulrike; Law, Rob; Fuchs, Matthias (editors): Information and Communication Technologies in Tourism 2010. Proceeding of the International Conference in Lugano, Switzerland, February 10-12, 2010, Wien 2010 (online resource of the Deutsche Nationalbibliothek Frankfurt/Germany)

Hänssler, Karl Heinz (editor): Management in der Hotellerie und Gastronomie. Betriebswirtschaftliche Grundlagen, München 2008

Hahn, Heinz; Kagelmann, H. Jürgen (editor): Tourismuspsychologie und Tourismussoziologie. Ein Handbuch zur Tourismuswissenschaft, München 1993

Hartmann, Rainer; Herwig, Michaela: „The best Job in the World" vs. "Die Botschafter der Ostfriesischen Inseln" – Social Media als neues Marketing Tool im Tourismus, in: Boksberger et al. 2011, p. 79-91

Höflich, Joachim: Opinion Leader, in: Hahn et al. 1993, p. 184-189

Hoschka, Peter: The Social Web Research Program, n.n. 1998, http://www.fit.fhg.de/~hoschka/Social%20Web.htm, accessed on 03.03.2011

Huber, Melanie: Kommunikation im Web 2.0, 2nd edition, Konstanz 2010

IBM (editor): developerWorks Interviews: Tim Berners-Lee, n.n., http://www.ibm.com/developerworks/podcast/dwi/cm-int082206txt.html, accessed on 21.10.2012

IHA: Hotelmarkt Deutschland 2011, Bonn 2011

Impulse4Travel (editor): Manifest aus 25 Thesen, n.n. 2012, http://www.impulse-4travel.de/, accessed on 01.09.2012

Internet World Business (editor): 40 Prozent der Klicks auf mobile Werbung sind nutzlos, n.n. 2012, http://www.internetworld.de/Nachrichten/Mobile/Zahlen-Studien/Trademob-Studie-40-Prozent-der-Klicks-auf-mobile-Werbung-sind-nutzlos-69378.html, accessed on 15.09.2012

iTronix (editor): Social Media & Hotels Studie 2011. Studienbericht. n.n. 2011, http://www.i-tronix.at/social-media-hotels-studie-2011/social-media-hotels-studie-studienbericht-2011.pdf, accessed on 28.08.2012

Ip, Crystal; Qi, ShanShan: Law, Rob: Which Overseas Destinations do Chinese Travelers Like to Visit, in: Gretzel et al. 2010, p. 345-356

Jacob, Rüdiger; Heinz, Andreas; Décieux, Jean Philippe; Eirmbter, Willy: Umfrage. Einführung in die Methoden der Umfrageforschung, 2nd edition, München 2011

Janßen, Julia; Thimm, Caja: Senioren im Social Web – entgrenztes Alter?, in: Thimm 2011, p. 375-395

Jiang, Jingxian; Gretzel, Ulrike; Law, Rob: Do Negative Experiences always lead to Dissatisfaction? – Testing Attribution Theory in the Context of Online Travel Review, in: Gretzel et al. 2010, p. 297-308

Kagermeier, Andreas: Social Web & Tourismus – Implikationen des internetgestützten Empfehlungsmarketing für die nachfrageseitige touristische Praxis, in: Boksberger et al. 2011, p. 59-78

Katona, George: Die Macht des Verbrauchers, Düsseldorf 1962

Kielholz, Annette: Online-Kommunikation. Die Psychologie der neuen Medien für die Berufspraxis. Heidelberg 2008

Knappe, Martin; Kracklauer, Alexander: Verkaufschance Web 2.0, Wiesbaden 2007

Koch, Michael; Richter, Alexander: Enterprise 2.0. Planung, Einführung und erfolgreicher Einsatz von Social Software in Unternehmen, 2nd edition, München 2009

Kotler, Philip; Keller, Kevin Lane; Bliemel; Friedhelm (a): Marketing-Management. Strategien für wertschaffendes Handeln, 12th edition, München 2007

Kotler Philip; Armstrong, Gary; Saunders, John; Wong, Veronica (b): Grundlagen des Marketing, 4th edition, München 2007

Kuß, Alfred; Tomczak, Torsten: Käuferverhalten. Eine marketingorientierte Einführung, 4th edition, Stuttgart 2008

Kuß, Alfred; Tomczak, Torsten: Käuferverhalten. Eine marketingorientierte Einführung, 2nd edition, Stuttgart 2000

Lassnig, Markus; Reich, Siegfried (editors): eTourismus, Heidelberg 2010

Lassnig, Markus: Von eTourism zu Travel 2.0 – IKT-Innovationen im Wechselbeispiel mit touristischen Trends, in: Lassnig et al. 2010, p. 6-18

Law, Rob; Fuchs, Matthias; Ricci, Francesco: Information and Communication Technologies in Tourism 2011. Proceedings of the International Conference in Innsbruck, Austria, January 26-28, 2011, Wien 2011 (online resource of the Deutsche Nationalbibliothek Frankfurt/Germany)

Marchiori, Elena; Eynard, Davide; Inversini, Alessandro; Cantoni, Lorenzo; Cerretti, Francesco: Harvesting Online Contents: An Analysis of Hotel Review Websites, in: Law et al. 2011, p. 101-112

Maurer, Christian; Schaich, Sabrina: Online Customer Reviews Used as Complaint Management Tool, in: Law et al. 2011, p. 499-510

Meffert, Heribert: Marketing. Grundlagen marktorientierter Unternehmensführung, 9th edition, Wiesbaden 2000

Mendes-Filho, Luiz; Tan, Felix B; Milne, Simone: Backpacker Use of User-Generated Content: A Consumer Empowerment Study, in: Gretzel et al. 2010, p. 455-466

Meyen, Michael; Pfaff-Rüdiger, Senta (editors): Internet im Alltag: qualitative Studien zum praktischen Sinn von Onlineangeboten, Berlin 2009

Nielsen, Jakob: Participation inequality: Encouraging More Users to Contribute, n.n. 2006, http://www.useit.com/alertbox/participation_inequality.html, accessed on 15.10.2011

O'Reilly Radar (editor): Web 2.0 Compact Definition?, n.n. 2005, http://radar.oreilly.com/2005/10/web-20-compact-definition.html, accessed on 15.10.2011

O'Reilly Verlag (editor): Web 2.0 zum Mitmachen. Die beliebtesten Anwendungen, Köln 2007

Pfaff-Rüdiger, Senta; Dudenhöffer, Kathrin; Huss, Julia; Meyen, Michael : „Dort bekomme ich alles". Internetnutzung im Alltag, in: Meyen et al. 2009, p. 41-85

Porst, Rolf: Fragebogen. Ein Arbeitsbuch. Studienskripte zur Soziologie, 3rd edition, Wiesbaden 2011

Prensky, Marc: Digital Natives, Digital Immigrants, n.n. 2001, http://www.marcprensky.com/writing/Prensky%20-%20Digital%20Natives,%20Digital%20Immigrants%20-%20Part1.pdf, accessed on 20.08.2011

Quack, Heinz-Dieter; Schreiber, Birke: Die Freizeit- und Tourismuswirtschaft in Deutschland – ein Überblick, in: Becker et al. 2003, p. 357-370

Raab, Fanny: Das Social Web im Städtetourismus. Eine Untersuchung der Auswirkungen auf Informationsverhalten und räumliche Verhaltensmuster unter besonderer Berücksichtigung von Nischenangeboten, Trier 2012, http://ubt.opus.hbz-nrw.de/volltexte/2013/782/pdf/Dissertation_FannyRaab_Social_Web_im_StAdtetourismus_2012.pdf

Reevo: Bad reviews are good for business. The power of negative reviews, n.n. 2012, http://www.reevoo.com/resources/ebooks/bad-reviews-are-good-business, accessed on 15.09.2012

Reisenzahn, Thomas: Webmarketing in der Hotellerie: Nutzung und Erfolgsfaktoren für den Einsatz, in: Lassnig et al. 2010, p. 29-36

Riegler, Barbara; Stangl, Brigitte: Monitoring Web 2.0 – User Generated Content in der Hotellerie im deutschsprachigen Raum, in: Boksberger et al. 2011, p. 105-117

Schegg, Roland; Fux, Michael: A Comparative Analysis of Content in Traditional Survey versus Hotel Review Websites, in: Gretzel et al. 2010, p. 429-454

Simons, Anton: Journalismus 2.0, Konstanz 2011

Social Media Akademie (editor): 5 Gründe warum Facebook 2012 verschwinden wird, n.n. 2012, http://community.socialmediaakademie.de/2012/08/24/5-grunde-warum-facebook-verschwinden-wird/, accessed on 01.09.2012

Sturm, Sabrina: Web 2.0 and the Health Care Market, Hamburg 2010

Süddeutsche.de (editor): Wie man Internetnutzer zum Sprechen bringt, n.n. 2012, http://www.sueddeutsche.de/digital/privatsphaere-im-social-web-wie-man-internetnutzer-zum-sprechen-bringt-1.1441039, accessed on 15.09.2012

Thimm, Caja (editor): Social Media. Theorie und Praxis digitaler Sozialität, Frankfurt 2011

TIME Magazine (editor): Person of the Year: You, n.n. 2006, http://www.time.com/time/covers/0,16641,1101061225,00.html., accessed on 15.07.2012

Tnooz.com (editor): Three times more people view TripAdvisor reviews on sites other than TripAdvisor, n.n. 2011, http://www.tnooz.com/2011/06/01/news/three-times-more-people-view-TripAdvisor-reviews-on-sites-other-than-TripAdvisor/, accessed on 20.08.2012

Tourismuszukunft (editor): "gtrot" – das neue "Where I've Been"?, n.n. 2011, http://www.tourismuszukunft.de/2011/02/gtrot-das-neue-where-ive-been/, accessed on 05.04.2011

TripAdvisor (editor): TripAdvisor Business Survey Reveals U.S. Hotels Optimistic on 2012 Economy, n.n. 2012, http://www.tripadvisor.com/PressCenter-i5056-c1-Press_Releases.html, accessed on 16.09.2012

TrustYou: Über TrustYou, n.n. 2012, http://www.trustyou.com/about_overview_de.html, accessed on 01.08.2012

Van Eimeren, Birgit; Frees, Beate: 76 Prozent der Deutschen online – neue Nutzungssituation durch mobile Endgeräte, in: Media Perspektiven 7-8/2012, p. 362-379, n.n. 2012, http://www.media-perspektiven.de/uploads/tx_mppublications/0708-2012_Eimeren_Frees_01.pdf, accessed on 01.09.2012

VIR (editor): Daten und Fakten zum Online Reisemarkt 2012, n.n. 2012, http://www.v-i-r.de/download-mafo-datenfakten/df-2012-web.pdf, accessed on 16.09.2012

VIR (editor): Daten und Fakten zum Online Reisemarkt 2011, n.n. 2011, http://www.v-i-r.de/download-mafo-datenfakten/2011-df.pdf, accessed on 12.05.2011

VIR; Internationale Hochschule Bad Honnef-Bonn (editors): Untersuchung der Bedeutung und Glaubwürdigkeit von Bewertungen auf Internetportalen, n.n. 2011, http://www.v-i-r.de/download-mafo/Glaubw%C3%BCrdigkeit%20von%20Hotelbewertungen.pdf, accessed on 20.05.2012

Weinberg, Peter: Das Entscheidungsverhalten der Konsumenten, Paderborn 1981

Weltbevölkerung.de (editor): Länderdatenbank, n.n. 2012, http://www.weltbevoelkerung.de/oberes-menue/publikationen-downloads/zu-unseren-themen/laenderdatenbank.html?tx_aecountrydb_pi1[country]=161, accessed on 27.09.2012

Winter, Johannes: Neue Anwendungen und Geschäftsfelder im Web 2.0, in: Gehrke 2007, p. 75-90

Wöhler, Karlheinz: Informationsverhalten, in: Hahn et al. 1993, p. 155-160

Xiang, Zheng: Dynamic Social Media in Online Travel Information Search: A Preliminary Analysis, in: Law et al. 2011, p. 343–353

Zangerl, Teresa; Gattringer, Carina; Groth, Aleksander; Mirski, Peter: Silver Surfers & eTourism: Web usability and Testing Methods for the Generation 50plus, in: Law et al. 2011, p. 75-87

Appendix

A1: Exemplary Booking Widget: Best Western

Front page of the Facebook fan page:

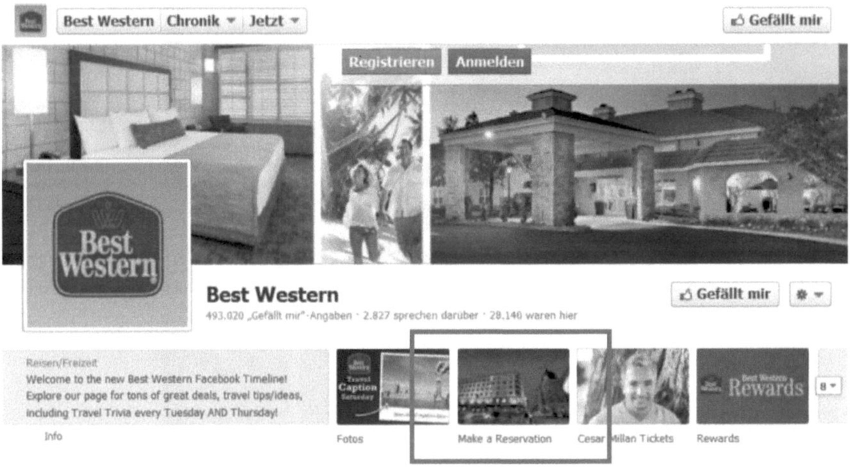

Source: Facebook[499]

499 Seen on: https://www.facebook.com/BestWestern?ref=ts&fref=ts (accessed on 22.11.2012)

Front page of booking widget:

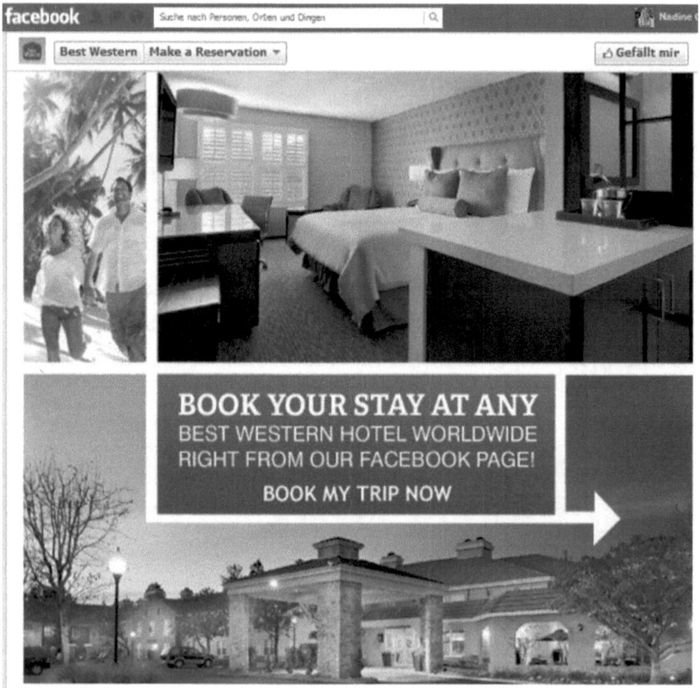

Source: Facebook[500]

500 Seen on: https://www.facebook.com/BestWestern/app_281788675224892 (accessed on 22.11.2012)

Actual booking widget:

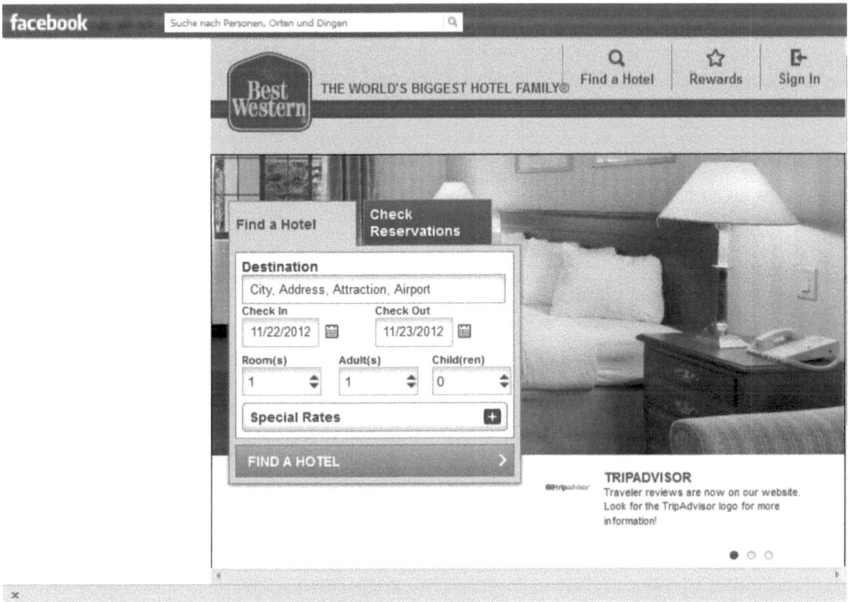

Source: Facebook[501]

501 Seen on: https://apps.facebook.com/bestwesternbooking/ (accessed on 22.11.2012)

A2: TripAdvisor Widget

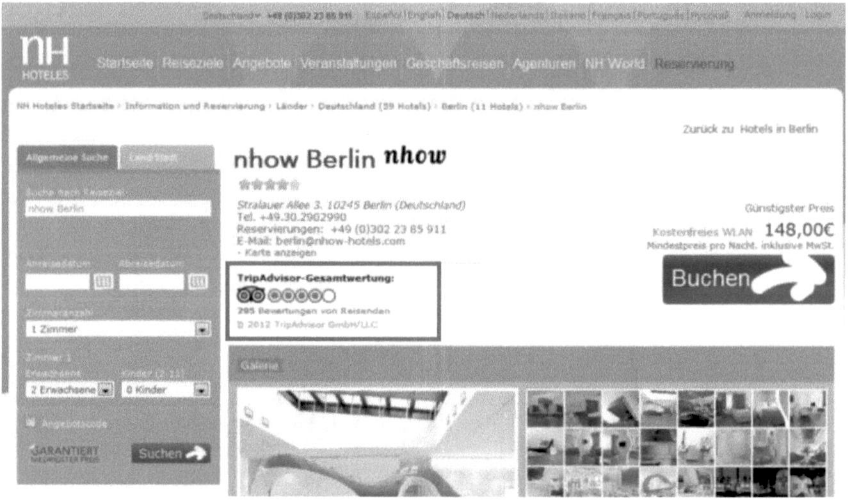

Source: NH Hoteles[502]

502 Seen on: http://www.nh-hotels.de/nh/de/hotels/deutschland/berlin/nhow-berlin.html (accessed on 22.11.2012)

A3: Questionnaire

Welcome page:

Sehr geehrte Damen und Herren,

im Auftrag untersuche ich in Zusammenarbeit mit der Universität Trier die Auswirkungen des Internets auf die Hotelsuche.

Die Befragung wird Sie maximal 10 Minuten in Anspruch nehmen. Als Dankeschön verlosen wir unter allen Teilnehmern ein Hotel Ihrer Wahl. Die attraktiven Leistungen dieses besonderen Angebots finden Sie hier

Selbstverständlich wird diese Umfrage anonym ausgewertet und der Datenschutz zu jedem Zeitpunkt vollumfänglich beachtet.

Sollten Sie Fragen oder Anregungen haben, können Sie mir gerne jederzeit eine E-Mail an schicken.

Vielen Dank für Ihre Mithilfe.

Herzliche Grüße

Nadine Chehimi
Externe Doktorandin Universität Trier

Weiter

Questions about the general travel behaviour:

Wie viele Hotelaufenthalte haben Sie durchschnittlich pro Jahr?

○ 1 - 2 ○ 3 - 4 ○ mehr als 4

Sind diese Hotelaufenthalte überwiegend

○ privat? ○ geschäftlich?

Wie buchen Sie Ihren Hotelaufenthalt in der Regel? (Mehrfachnennungen möglich)

☐ telefonisch im Hotel ☐ per E-Mail im Hotel ☐ Reisebüro ☐ online über die Hotelhomepage ☐ online über Drittanbieter, z.B. hrs.de ☐ andere

Nutzen Sie ein Smartphone oder Tablet PC zur Buchung?

○ ja ○ nein

Wie haben Sie Ihren letzten Hotelaufenthalt gebucht?

○ telefonisch im Hotel ○ per E-Mail im Hotel ○ Reisebüro ○ online über die Hotelhomepage ○ online über Drittanbieter, z.B. hrs.de ○ andere

Weiter

Questions about the general Internet usage and social web knowledge:

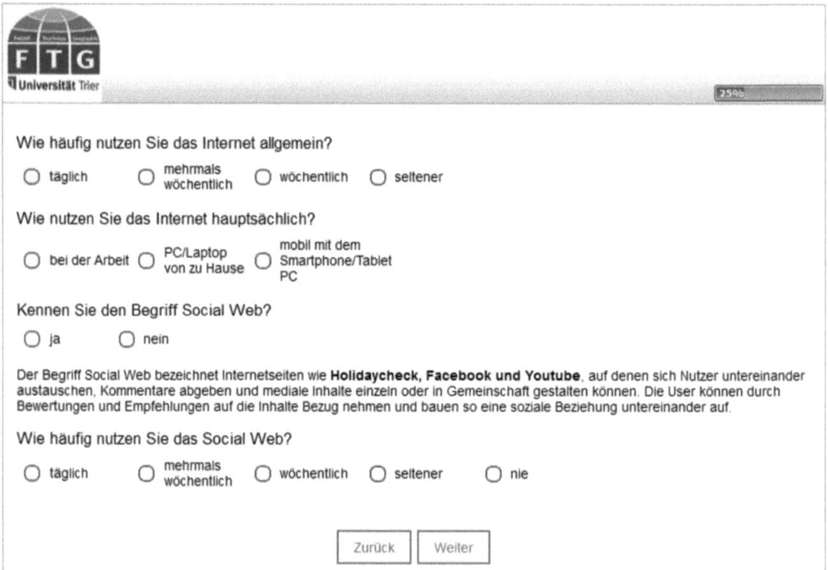

FTG
Universität Trier
25%

Wie häufig nutzen Sie das Internet allgemein?

○ täglich ○ mehrmals wöchentlich ○ wöchentlich ○ seltener

Wie nutzen Sie das Internet hauptsächlich?

○ bei der Arbeit ○ PC/Laptop von zu Hause ○ mobil mit dem Smartphone/Tablet PC

Kennen Sie den Begriff Social Web?

○ ja ○ nein

Der Begriff Social Web bezeichnet Internetseiten wie **Holidaycheck, Facebook und Youtube**, auf denen sich Nutzer untereinander austauschen, Kommentare abgeben und mediale Inhalte einzeln oder in Gemeinschaft gestalten können. Die User können durch Bewertungen und Empfehlungen auf die Inhalte Bezug nehmen und bauen so eine soziale Beziehung untereinander auf.

Wie häufig nutzen Sie das Social Web?

○ täglich ○ mehrmals wöchentlich ○ wöchentlich ○ seltener ○ nie

Zurück Weiter

Questions about the general social web usage:

FTG
Universität Trier
33%

In welchem Maße nutzen Sie die folgenden Social Web Seiten?

	täglich	mehrmals wöchentlich	wöchentlich	seltener	nie	noch nie gehört
Hotelbewertungsseiten, z.B. Holidaycheck	○	○	○	○	○	○
Soziale Netzwerke, z.B. Facebook	○	○	○	○	○	○
Video- und Fotoportale, z.B. Youtube	○	○	○	○	○	○
Blogs und Podcasts	○	○	○	○	○	○
Microblogs, z.B. Twitter	○	○	○	○	○	○
Reisecommunities, z.B. Trips by Tips	○	○	○	○	○	○
Buchungsseiten mit Bewertungsfunktion, z.B. hrs.de	○	○	○	○	○	○

Zurück Weiter

Online and offline information search:

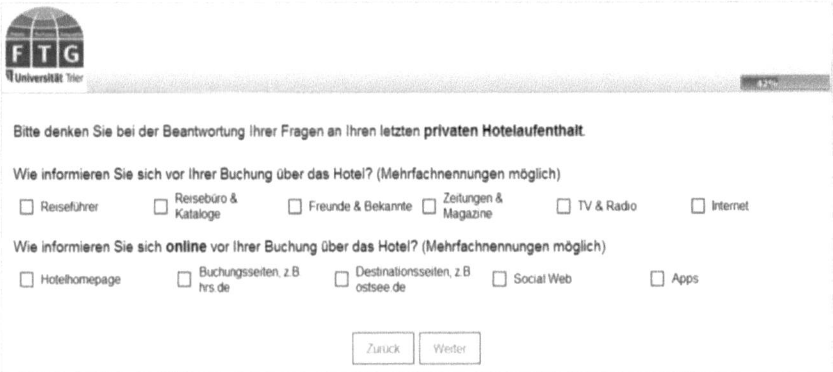

FTG Universität Trier

42%

Bitte denken Sie bei der Beantwortung Ihrer Fragen an Ihren letzten **privaten Hotelaufenthalt**.

Wie informieren Sie sich vor Ihrer Buchung über das Hotel? (Mehrfachnennungen möglich)

☐ Reiseführer ☐ Reisebüro & Kataloge ☐ Freunde & Bekannte ☐ Zeitungen & Magazine ☐ TV & Radio ☐ Internet

Wie informieren Sie sich **online** vor Ihrer Buchung über das Hotel? (Mehrfachnennungen möglich)

☐ Hotelhomepage ☐ Buchungsseiten, z.B. hrs.de ☐ Destinationsseiten, z.B. ostsee.de ☐ Social Web ☐ Apps

Zurück Weiter

Social web usage during the last information search:

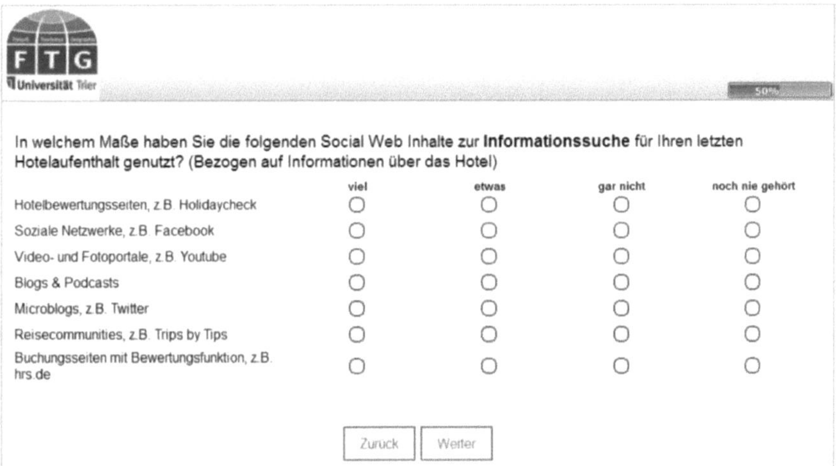

FTG Universität Trier

50%

In welchem Maße haben Sie die folgenden Social Web Inhalte zur **Informationssuche** für Ihren letzten Hotelaufenthalt genutzt? (Bezogen auf Informationen über das Hotel)

	viel	etwas	gar nicht	noch nie gehört
Hotelbewertungsseiten, z.B. Holidaycheck	○	○	○	○
Soziale Netzwerke, z.B. Facebook	○	○	○	○
Video- und Fotoportale, z.B. Youtube	○	○	○	○
Blogs & Podcasts	○	○	○	○
Microblogs, z.B. Twitter	○	○	○	○
Reisecommunities, z.B. Trips by Tips	○	○	○	○
Buchungsseiten mit Bewertungsfunktion, z.B. hrs.de	○	○	○	○

Zurück Weiter

Questions about the influence of the social web:

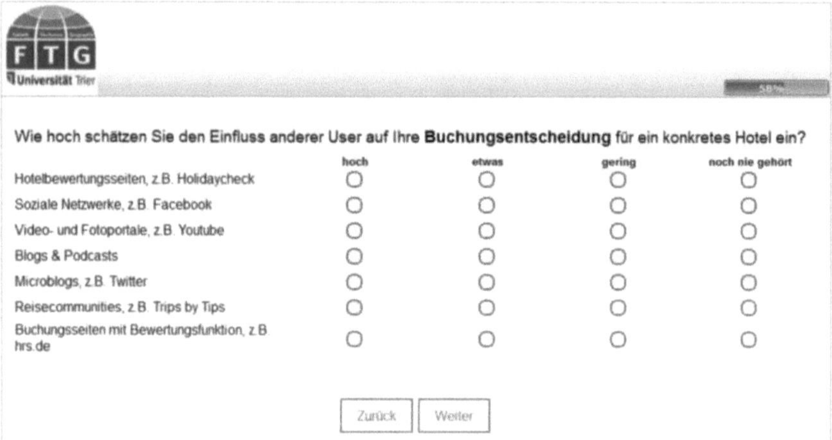
FTG
Universität Trier

58%

Wie hoch schätzen Sie den Einfluss anderer User auf Ihre Buchungsentscheidung für ein konkretes Hotel ein?

	hoch	etwas	gering	noch nie gehört
Hotelbewertungsseiten, z.B. Holidaycheck	○	○	○	○
Soziale Netzwerke, z.B. Facebook	○	○	○	○
Video- und Fotoportale, z.B. Youtube	○	○	○	○
Blogs & Podcasts	○	○	○	○
Microblogs, z.B. Twitter	○	○	○	○
Reisecommunities, z.B. Trips by Tips	○	○	○	○
Buchungsseiten mit Bewertungsfunktion, z.B. hrs.de	○	○	○	○

Zurück Weiter

Questions about advertising and booking possibilities:

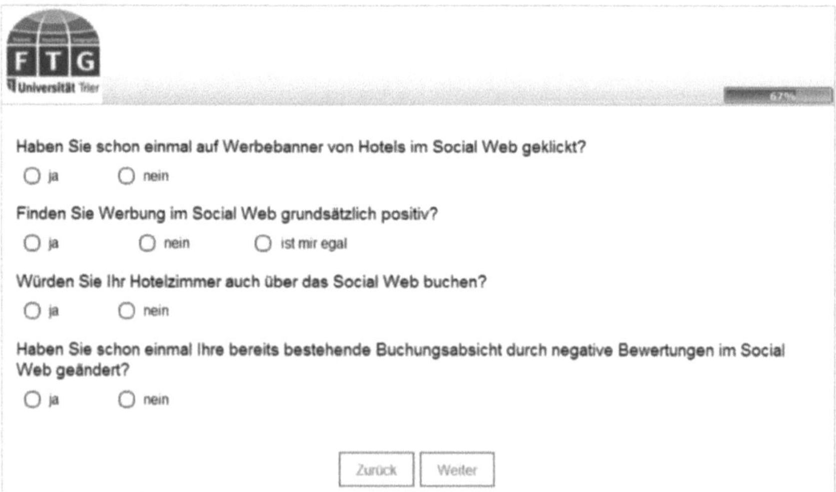
FTG
Universität Trier

67%

Haben Sie schon einmal auf Werbebanner von Hotels im Social Web geklickt?

○ ja ○ nein

Finden Sie Werbung im Social Web grundsätzlich positiv?

○ ja ○ nein ○ ist mir egal

Würden Sie Ihr Hotelzimmer auch über das Social Web buchen?

○ ja ○ nein

Haben Sie schon einmal Ihre bereits bestehende Buchungsabsicht durch negative Bewertungen im Social Web geändert?

○ ja ○ nein

Zurück Weiter

Questions about the personal social web reporting:

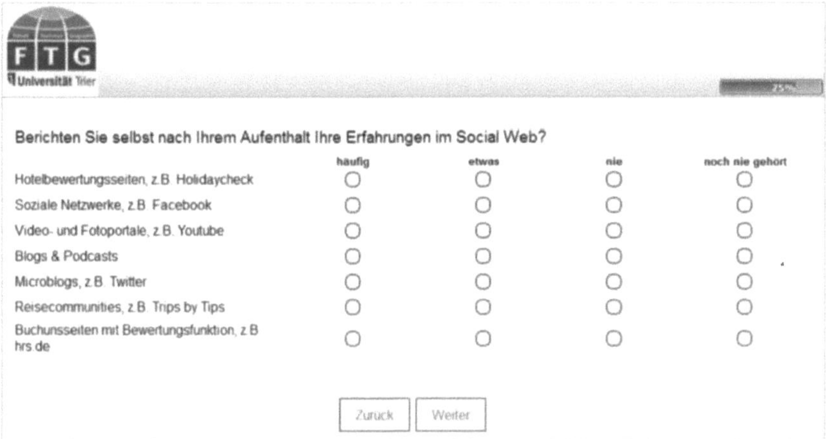

FTG Universität Trier

75%

Berichten Sie selbst nach Ihrem Aufenthalt Ihre Erfahrungen im Social Web?

	häufig	etwas	nie	noch nie gehört
Hotelbewertungsseiten, z.B. Holidaycheck	○	○	○	○
Soziale Netzwerke, z.B. Facebook	○	○	○	○
Video- und Fotoportale, z.B. Youtube	○	○	○	○
Blogs & Podcasts	○	○	○	○
Microblogs, z.B. Twitter	○	○	○	○
Reisecommunities, z.B. Trips by Tips	○	○	○	○
Buchunsseiten mit Bewertungsfunktion, z.B. hrs.de	○	○	○	○

Zurück Weiter

Questions about the use of the hotel company's Facebook and Twitter site:

FTG Universität Trier

83%

Im Social Web suchen Sie Informationen zu folgenden Aspekten des Hotels

	häufig	etwas	nie
Lage	○	○	○
Service	○	○	○
Essen	○	○	○
Zimmer	○	○	○
Angebote	○	○	○
News	○	○	○

Sind Sie Mitglied der Facebook Fanpage?

○ ja ○ nein

Folgen Sie auf Twitter?

○ ja ○ nein

Zurück Weiter

Questions about demographic characteristics:

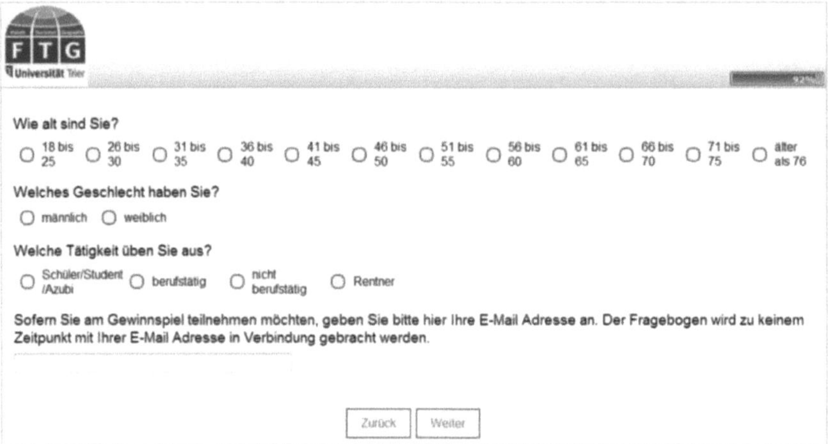

F T G
Universität Trier

92%

Wie alt sind Sie?

○ 18 bis 25 ○ 26 bis 30 ○ 31 bis 35 ○ 36 bis 40 ○ 41 bis 45 ○ 46 bis 50 ○ 51 bis 55 ○ 56 bis 60 ○ 61 bis 65 ○ 66 bis 70 ○ 71 bis 75 ○ älter als 76

Welches Geschlecht haben Sie?

○ männlich ○ weiblich

Welche Tätigkeit üben Sie aus?

○ Schüler/Student /Azubi ○ berufstätig ○ nicht berufstätig ○ Rentner

Sofern Sie am Gewinnspiel teilnehmen möchten, geben Sie bitte hier Ihre E-Mail Adresse an. Der Fragebogen wird zu keinem Zeitpunkt mit Ihrer E-Mail Adresse in Verbindung gebracht werden.

Zurück Weiter

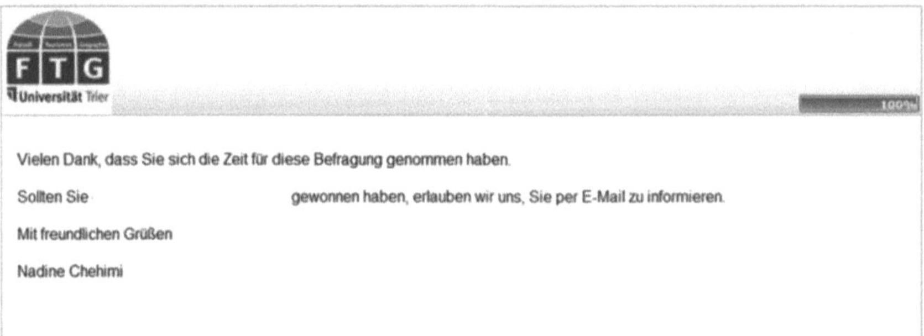

F T G
Universität Trier

100%

Vielen Dank, dass Sie sich die Zeit für diese Befragung genommen haben.

Sollten Sie gewonnen haben, erlauben wir uns, Sie per E-Mail zu informieren.

Mit freundlichen Grüßen

Nadine Chehimi

Source: own survey

A4: Age and Gender Pyramid of the Sample Group

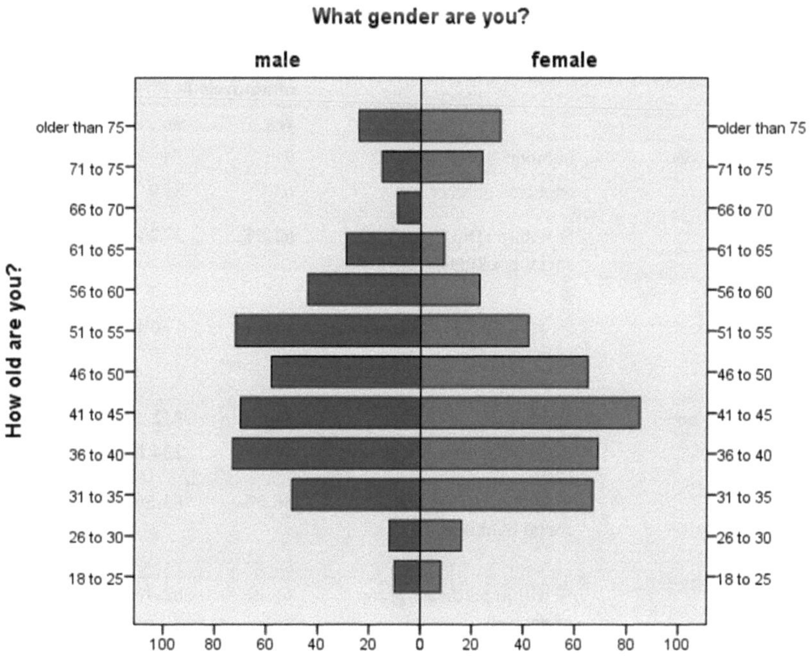

Source: own survey

A5: Expected Cross Tabulation: Social Bookings Affinity and Informational Social Web Usage

			predicted group of analysis 1		
			yes	**no**	**total**
Would you book your hotel room via the social web?	**yes**	number	91	54	145
		expected number	63.1	81.9	145
		% within affinity towards social bookings	**62.8%**	37.2%	100%
		% within predicted group of analysis 1	38.6%	17.6%	26.8%
	no	number	145	252	397
		expected number	172.9	224.1	397
		% within affinity towards social bookings	36.5%	**63.50%**	100%
		% within predicted group of analysis 1	61.4%	82.4%	73.2%
total		number	236	306	542
		expected number	236	306	542
		% within affinity towards social bookings	43.5%	56.5%	100%
		% within predicted group of analysis 1	100%	100%	100%

Source: own survey

A6: Exemplary Social Advertising

Source: Facebook[503]

Source: TripAdvisor[504]

503 Seen on: http://www.facebook.com (accessed on 22.11.2012)

504 Seen on: http://www.tripadvisor.de (accessed on 22.11.2012)

A7: Expected Cross Tabulation: Perception of Social Advertising and Informational Social Web Usage

			predicted group of analysis 1			total
			positive	negative	indiffe-rent	
perception of social advertising	**positive**	number	38	47	14	99
		expected number	21.0	48.9	29.1	99.0
		% within perception of social advertising	**38.4%**	47.5%	14.1%	100.0%
		% within predicted group of analysis 1	33.0%	17.6%	8.8%	18.3%
	negative	number	29	105	60	194
		expected number	41.2	95.7	57.0	194.0
		% within perception of social advertising	14.9%	**54.1%**	30.9%	100.0%
		% within predicted group of analysis 1	25.2%	39.3%	37.7%	35.9%
	indifferent	number	48	115	85	248
		expected number	52.7	122.4	72.9	248.0
		% within perception of social advertising	19.4%	46.4%	**34.3%**	100.0%
		% within predicted group of analysis 1	41.7%	43.1%	53.5%	45.8%
total		number	115	267	159	541
		expected number	115.0	267.0	159.0	541.0
		% within perception of social advertising	21.3%	49.4%	29.4%	100.0%
		% within predicted group of analysis 1	100.0%	100.0%	100.0%	100.0%

Source: own survey

Lebenslauf der Verfasserin

Persönliche Daten

Name	Nadine Lara Chehimi
Geburtsdatum und -ort	29.12.1984, Frankfurt am Main

Schulische Ausbildung

08/1995 bis 06/2004	Freiherr-vom-Stein Schule, Frankfurt am Main Abschluss: Abitur

Akademische Ausbildung

09/2004 bis 09/2007	Berufsakademie Rhein-Main Studiengang: Wirtschaft, Fachrichtung Hotel- und Gastronomiemanagement (Diplom-Betriebswirtin BA)
09/2007 bis 09/2009	Hochschule Heilbronn Studiengang: International Tourism Management (M.A. FH)
10/2010 bis 02/2013	Universität Trier externes Promotionsstudium (Dr. phil.)

MIX
Papier aus verantwortungsvollen Quellen
Paper from responsible sources
FSC® C105338

If you have any concerns about our products,
you can contact us on
ProductSafety@springernature.com

In case Publisher is established outside the EU,
the EU authorized representative is:
Springer Nature Customer Service Center GmbH
Europaplatz 3, 69115 Heidelberg, Germany

Printed by Libri Plureos GmbH
in Hamburg, Germany